The Girls' Guide to Life

How to Take Charge of the Issues That Affect You

by Catherine Dee

With illustrations by Cynthia Jabar
and photographs by Carol Palmer

Little, Brown and Company
Boston New York Toronto London

To John Javna

The photographer wishes to acknowledge the following organizations for their cooperation: Model Mugging of Boston; Boston Police; and Artists for Humanity, Boston.

Additional illustrations:
© Jan Eliot, pp. 23, 106
© Marian Henley, pp. 7, 37, 85
"Baton" from *The Fun House* by Lynda Barry. Copyright © 1987, 1986, 1985, 1984 by Lynda Barry. Reprinted by permission of HarperCollins Publishers, Inc.
"Look Guys" by Mike Peters. Reprinted by permission of Tribune Media Services.
Lisa Simpson frame from "Simpsons Comics #3" © 1996 Bongo Entertainments, Inc. Reprinted by permission of Bongo Comics Group. The Simpsons TM & © Twentieth Century Fox Film Corporation.

First Edition

Acknowledgments for copyrighted text material appear on page 146.

Library of Congress Cataloging-in-Publication Data
Dee, Catherine.
 The girls' guide to life : how to take charge of the issues that affect you / by Catherine Dee ; with illustrations by Cynthia Jabar and photographs by Carol Palmer.—1st ed.
  p.   cm.
Includes bibliographical references and index.
Summary: Uses information, activities, and creative writing to examine a variety of issues important to teenage girls, including how they are treated at home and at school, what they think of their bodies, sexual harassment, pay equity, and more.
 ISBN 0-316-17952-3
 1. Girls—United States—Juvenile literature. 2. Teenage girls—United States—Juvenile literature. 3. Sex role—United States—Juvenile literature. 4. Sexism—United States—Juvenile literature. 5. Women's rights—United States—Juvenile literature. 6. Feminism—United States—Juvenile literature. [1. Feminism. 2. Teenage girls—Conduct of life. 3. Sex role. 4. Self-perception.] I. Title.
HQ798.D397 1997
305.42´ 0973—dc20   96-27958

10 9   8   7   6   5   4

Q-KP

Published simultaneously in Canada by Little, Brown & Company (Canada) Limited

Printed in the United States of America

For bulk sales, contact your local bookstore or Little, Brown and Company Special Sales Department at (212) 522-8072.

Thanks!

This book was created with the help and support of many great people:

✪ The team at Little, Brown: Megan Shaw Tingley, my editor, who loved the concept and helped nurture it to reality; Erica Lombard Stahler; and everyone else who provided direction and guidance

✪ Fran Drake, my mother, who gave me a copy of Marlo Thomas's girl-affirming book *Free to Be . . . You & Me* when I was six; Orson Dee, my father, who cautioned me not to be *too* free; and Alan Javurek, my stepfather, who taught me that there is a middle ground

✪ John Javna, who taught me how to write a book

✪ The adults who read the manuscript: Fran Drake, Pamela Lowrie, Sarah Dee, Ryan Dee, Warren Herr, Sherry Powell, Ben Calica, Richard Meynell, Brian McGinnis, Helen Grieco, Darren Burton, and Craig Bristol

✪ The girls who read the manuscript: Lenne Klingaman, Hannah Dibner, Reilly Dibner, Anitra Bussy, Danial Dunlap, Kelly O'Neill, and Rachel Pfeffer

✪ All those who provided stories about their experiences: Frances Conley, Brazley Daraja, Danial Dunlap, Andrea Floyd, Susan Gillette, Josh Haner, Anastasia Higginbotham, Brooke Hodess, Jane Garland Katz, Amanda Keller, Laurel King, Doug Kirkpatrick, Brooke LeBaron, Marie G. Lee, Ann Richards, Jody Rohlena, Gloria Steinem, Barbara Stretchberry, Jasmine Victoria, Lauren Wales, and Roz Warren

✪ The people and organizations who served as resources or helped me compile information, including: Fiona Gow, my research assistant; Joe Kelly, Nancy Gruver, and Tya Ward, *New Moon;* Anastasia Higginbotham, Mary Maschino, Lisa Jacobs, and Suzie Bohnett, Girls Incorporated; Amy Richards and Barbara Findlen, *Ms.;* Jodi Grossblatt, the *Ms.* Foundation; Nan Stein, Wellesley College Center for Research on Women; Tracy Raasch and Connie Willegal, Girl Scouts/Illinois Crossroads Council; Joline Godfrey and Lynn Karlson, An Income of Her Own; Jan Stoltman, International Women's Writing Guild; Vivian Todini, NOW Legal Defense and Education Fund; Kathy Kleeman and Gilda Morales, Center for the American Woman and Politics; Betty Shepperd, Business and Professional Women USA; Amy Pretel, Long Island Fund for Women and Girls; Ann Simonton, Media Watch; Penny Paine, Resources for Girls and Young Women; George Dean, 50/50 by 2000; Joann Stemmerman, Circles of Courage; Nadia Moritz, Young Women's Project; Amy Kohut, Thompson Island Outward Bound; Feminist Majority Foundation; National Council for Research on Women; Fairness and Accuracy in Reporting; Center for Media Literacy; National Women's History Project; The Women's Sports Foundation; Christine Choy; Judy Logan; Donna Guthrie; Sherry Hagemann; Donnamarie K. Pignone; Mary Pipher; Peggy Orenstein; Emily Hancock; Lenna Lebovich; Brad Bunnin; Anna Billings; Sam Clemons; Paul Giusti; and Jessie Langer

Contents

Why Should Girls Care?

Do you ever find yourself:

✡ Keeping your thoughts to yourself for fear that someone won't like you because of what you have to say?
✡ Watching TV commercials for kids' games and being annoyed by the way boys always win?
✡ Repeatedly raising your hand in class—only to have the teacher call on the boy next to you?
✡ Wondering when there'll be a woman president?
✡ Feeling insecure about the way you look?
✡ Getting stuck doing more housework than your brother?
✡ Being intimidated by guys whistling at you or making disgusting comments?
✡ Playing on a coed sports team but being left out of the action?

If you answered yes to any of these questions, this book is for you. It's meant to help you cope with what it means to be a girl in America.

I wrote it because when I was growing up, I could have used a book like this! When I played coed soccer in ninth-grade P.E., I could run just as fast as the boys on my team and was often open to receive the ball, but the boys wouldn't kick it to me. I spent a lot of time feeling frustrated, because I could have scored plenty of goals. In addition, I didn't have an "hourglass" figure like the women I saw on TV and in magazines, and that made me feel that I didn't measure up. And although I knew I was smart and had meaningful things to say, I was reluctant to express myself too much for fear of what people would think of an outspoken, opinionated girl.

If I had known then some of the things I know now—like the fact that boys may ignore girls in P.E. because they feel insecure, that 95 percent of women and girls don't look like the models on TV, and that girls are conditioned by our culture not to be too outspoken—I might have felt different or responded differently to situations in my life. But even though I couldn't read a book like that, I got to write one, so now maybe you'll be better prepared.

Of course, thanks to the dedication of women activists, things have improved considerably since I was growing up. Adults are now more aware of the challenges girls face in our world. Make no mistake: This book is intended to celebrate the progress made by women and girls up to this point. On the other hand, it's still likely that you'll have to deal with some of the issues discussed in this book, either now or when you are older. Girls didn't cause the problem of gender bias and are not responsible for fixing it. However, you can do a lot—both for yourself and for the female half of the population—even just by being informed. The more you understand what's happening, the better prepared you'll be to handle a variety of situations in ways that make you feel good.

The Girls' Guide to Life doesn't tell you everything there is to know about this subject, but it's a start. Since every girl has her own unique life and can probably relate to some people's experiences more than others, I've included real-life stories from lots of different people. I contacted women and girls all over the country—some who were professional writers and some who didn't even know they could write—and got back many inspiring tales. I've also included work sheets, suggestions for handling various challenges, lists of books and publications for you to read, and names of relevant organizations.

So the next time you're in a situation where you feel that something isn't fair, don't despair. As they say, knowledge is power, and when you know what's going on, you can make informed, self-respecting decisions. If you get in the habit of approaching situations this way, you will help make a good name for girls everywhere, letting the world know they deserve respect. More important, you will greatly increase your chances for real happiness and success!

Hope you like the book!

Catherine Dee

"Never doubt that a small group of thoughtful, concerned citizens can change the world. Indeed, it is the only thing that ever has."

—Margaret Mead, anthropologist

A QUICK QUIZ
WOMEN'S ISSUES: DEFINING TERMS

1. What is the women's movement?
   a. A giant group of female immigrants making its way to the United States
   b. The push to achieve equality for women and girls
   c. A new kind of dance

2. What is a feminist?
   a. Someone who supports equal political, economic, and social rights for everybody
   b. Someone who wants women to take over the earth
   c. A woman who wears a lot of frilly clothes and makeup

3. What is gender bias?
   a. When girls wish they had the advantages boys have
   b. Favoring one age group
   c. Favoring boys or girls

4. Which of these is an example of gender bias?
   a. A man doing the dishes
   b. A teacher choosing only boys for a class project
   c. Inviting only certain girlfriends to a party

5. What does ERA stand for?
   a. Expect random acts.
   b. End racism altogether.
   c. Equal Rights Amendment

6. Which of these is an example of sexual harassment?
   a. Being told someone has a crush on you
   b. Being told by your parents you can't date till you're fifteen
   c. Having someone snap your bra strap

7. Which of these is a stereotype—a generally believed idea that isn't always true?
   a. Only females can bear children.
   b. Many girls grow up to become scientists.
   c. Boys are better than girls at math.

LIFE IN AMERICA

8. In this country women generally make less _____ than men.
   a. Money
   b. Cake
   c. Time for their families

9. When an American woman gets married, it's traditional for her to:

a. Wear a short red dress

b. Walk down the aisle by herself

c. Give up her last name and take her new husband's

10. Which of these is an organization that fights gender bias?

a. Greenpeace

b. Girls Incorporated

c. The Lions Club

11. As of 1997, women made up _____ percent of those in the U.S. Congress.

a. 48

b. 11

c. There are women in Congress?

12. When did the modern-day American women's movement formally start?

a. When the men's movement accomplished its goals

b. When Susan B. Anthony's brothers left the toilet seat up and Susan fell in

c. When women won the right to vote

ANSWERS

1. b. For lack of a better term, this is the name of the ongoing struggle to gain equality for women and girls.

2. a. The term *feminist* has a bad rap in some circles as someone who hates men and wants to take power away from them, but this is not accurate. A feminist is simply a person of either gender who believes in equality for both genders.

3. c. Also referred to as sexism, gender bias is commonly directed at girls and women.

4. b. Gender bias is what it sounds like: discrimination against someone because of gender.

5. c. The ERA is a proposed constitutional amendment that would prohibit discrimination on the basis of gender. At press time for this book, it had not yet been approved.

6. c. Sexual harassment is unwanted sexually oriented comments or touching.

7. c. When it comes to math, boys do not have a genetic advantage; girls have the ability to do just as well.

8. a. On average, women earn less money—76 cents for each dollar men earn.

9. c. Women have traditionally changed their names to reflect virtual or symbolic ownership by their husbands. Wives are generally no longer seen this way, but the name-change tradition is still with us.

10. b. Girls Incorporated helps girls learn technical skills and find out about nontraditional careers.

11. b. A record 11 percent of Congress was female as of 1997.

12. c. American women fought for the right to vote for decades and finally achieved it in 1920. That year is considered the beginning of the movement.

Women's History Highlights

American women have been working to achieve equality since the country was founded. In the 1900s, they started making real progress. Here are some milestones.

1848: A meeting called the Seneca Falls Women's Rights Convention is held in New York State to discuss the need for women's equality.

1872: Victoria Woodhull forms her own political party and becomes the first woman to run for president of the United States. She loses to Ulysses S. Grant.

1910: The first International (Working) Women's Day is celebrated on March 8. It commemorates an 1857 demonstration for better working conditions for female garment and textile workers.

1916: Jeannette Rankin, a Democrat from Montana, is the first woman elected to the House of Representatives.

1920: After a long struggle for suffrage, American women win the right to vote when the Nineteenth Amendment to the Constitution is ratified.

1923: Alice Paul drafts the Equal Rights Amendment (ERA), a constitutional amendment stating that women must be treated equally.

1963: Congress passes the Equal Pay Act, which is supposed to guarantee that women have the same earning power as men in similar jobs.

In *The Feminine Mystique,* Betty Friedan argues that women need more than marriage and kids to be happy. The book becomes a bestseller.

1966: The National Organization for Women (NOW), the most prominent activist group for women, is founded.

1968: The first major demonstration for women's rights takes place at the Miss America Pageant. "Women's liberation" groups form as the female counterpart to the mostly male student activism movement.

The first national Women's Liberation Conference is held, helping women from thirty-seven states and Canada organize a plan of action.

1970: On the fiftieth anniversary of the ratification (approval) of the Nineteenth Amendment, more than one hundred thousand women participate in demonstrations.

1971: The National Women's Political Caucus is founded. Its goal: equal representation for women at all levels of the nation's political system. Today it has considerable influence, distributing hundreds of thousands of dollars to the campaigns of women running for office.

1972: *Ms.* magazine's first issue is published. Gloria Steinem, the most well known leader of the women's movement, is the editor.

The ERA is passed by the Senate and sent to the states to be ratified. However, too few states ratify it and it fails to be made into law.

1973: The Supreme Court's ruling in the case of *Roe v. Wade* upholds women's right to privacy as including the right to have first-trimester abortions in all states. Feminists hail the ruling because it ensures that women will have control over their own bodies.

1975: Title IX, a law that bans sex discrimination in college sports and increases opportunities for girls and women in sports, is passed.

1977: Janet Guthrie is the first woman to race in the famous Indianapolis 500.

1979: The Supreme Court rules in support of company policies that favor hiring and promoting women and minorities.

1980: Eight percent fewer women than men vote for Ronald Reagan. This is the first time that women as a group vote significantly differently from men in their choice for president. This phenomenon is named the "gender gap."

1981: Sandra Day O'Connor, at age fifty-one, is the first woman appointed to the Supreme Court.

1982: The ERA again fails to be ratified by the minimum number of states required.

1983: TV newscaster Christine Craft is fired because she is "too unattractive, too old, and not deferential enough to men." She responds by filing a lawsuit and wins five hundred thousand dollars.

Sally Ride becomes the first female astronaut, serving as mission specialist on the space shuttle *Challenger*'s second voyage.

A landmark wage discrimination case in Washington state is resolved in favor of women who weren't earning as much as men in comparable, or similar, jobs.

1984: Presidential candidate Walter Mondale chooses Geraldine Ferraro as his running mate, the first woman vice-presidential candidate for a major political party.

1987: The Supreme Court rules that male-only clubs discriminate against women. The Rotary, Lions, and Kiwanis Clubs let women join.

The Fund for the Feminist Majority, an education-oriented organization focused on women's issues, is founded.

1991: Susan Faludi's *Backlash: The War Against American Women,* which documents sexism in America, is published. It stays on the bestseller list for months.

Professor Anita Hill testifies before an all-male committee that Supreme Court nominee Clarence Thomas sexually harassed her. He is confirmed anyway, but her testimony brings the issue of sexual harassment into the mainstream.

1992: "The Year of the Woman." Women make up 54 percent of registered voters, meaning that there are ten million more women voters than men. A record number of women are elected (forty-seven in the House of Representatives and six in the Senate). Carol Moseley Braun of Illinois becomes the first African-American female senator.

The largest-ever women's march and rally (750,000 people) is held in Washington, D.C.

1993: Hillary Rodham Clinton leads the fight for health care reform, showing America that a first lady doesn't have to resign herself to stereotypical women's duties such as decorating and choosing White House china.

1995: The Supreme Court rules that public military schools can't discriminate against women, allowing Shannon Faulkner to become the first female cadet at the previously all-male Citadel.

1996: "The Year of the Woman at the Olympics." Women win nineteen of America's forty-four gold medals, and their Olympic events are prominently featured in television coverage.

Bill Clinton is reelected president thanks to the largest voting gender gap ever. Nine United States senators and fifty-one members of the House are women—an all-time record.

Personal Life

Chapter 1
Looking Out for #1

Think about your friends. Who's the most confident—the one who believes in herself the most, the one who's least afraid to say what's on her mind? She probably has high self-esteem.

What is self-esteem? "Confidence and satisfaction in oneself," according to *Webster's* dictionary. Psychologist Nathaniel Branden elaborates: "confidence in our ability to think, learn, choose, and make appropriate decisions . . . and in our right to be happy; confidence that achievement, success, friendship, respect, love, and fulfillment are appropriate to us." Your level of self-esteem determines how you feel about yourself and affects every aspect of your life. For example, a person with high self-esteem doesn't put herself down around her friends or let herself be treated badly by others.

Why does self-esteem merit a whole chapter in this book? Because our culture has traditionally supported the belief that girls and women aren't important and that their opinions don't matter that much. Of course, that isn't true, and high self-esteem helps a girl cope with society's attempts to "put her in her place." In order to stand up for your rights as a girl—and the rights of all girls and women—you need to know and believe that you deserve those rights.

The Turning Point

Research shows that girls gradually lose self-esteem as they reach adolescence. In elementary school, most girls have strong self-esteem and aren't afraid to voice their thoughts. But once they hit their teens, their self-confidence can go down the drain. They may not feel as self-assured, outspoken, or attractive; they may listen more instead of talking; and they may be more worried about what other people think of them. According to the American Association of University Women, in elementary school, 45 percent of girls and 55 percent of boys indicate that they have high self-esteem by saying they are "good at a lot of things." But in middle school, only 29 percent of girls say this, compared to 46 percent of boys.

Why would anyone change her self-confidence level so drastically? One reason is that when girls reach their teens, they are expected to become more mature and are pressured to conform to traditional gender roles. One role is the "self-sacrificer"—someone who consistently puts others' needs first. According to Carol Gilligan, who has done extensive research on girls and self-esteem, "Sensitivity to the needs of others and the assumption of responsibility for taking care [of others] lead women to attend to voices other than their own and to include in their judgment other points of view."

Girls Incorporated, an organization dedicated to helping girls with life planning, adds: "Girls are repeatedly rewarded for being polite, behaving well, and looking pretty," as opposed to expressing their thoughts, having opinions, and accomplishing things. As girls grow up, these social expectations continue to be reinforced. For example, a girl may think that adults or classmates will like her more if she doesn't have strong opinions, so she may keep her thoughts to herself, even if this means suppressing her basically talkative personality.

Whatever the causes, when the majority of girls enter public junior high school, their self-esteem shrinks. This can be seen in many ways. For instance, girls typically try not to appear too smart, since many boys feel threatened by intelligent girls and it's not considered cool to be brainy. "If a teacher asks a question, I'll often know the answer but I won't raise my hand because it would make me look like a nerd," says Sydney Bird, a seventh-grade girl in Berkeley, California. "Sometimes I do speak up without realizing it, but then I wonder whether I should have."

The Consequences

You may be thinking, What's the big deal? A girl can keep quiet yet still be smart and have her own opinions. Well, sort of. If you have been a quiet person all your life, then it's a natural state for you; if you haven't, it's probably not—you are, in effect, masking your true self, which may cause problems later. For example, when you graduate from high school, you may continue with your quiet pattern but find that college pro-

4

fessors and potential employers want you to act more confident, "think out loud," and not be afraid to voice your opinions. Or you may find that you have trouble in relationships because you don't ask for what you want. Or you may choose not to do something challenging because you have learned not to expect too much of yourself. Or you may deserve a raise at work but not feel comfortable asking for it.

So you see, it *is* a big deal! Your self-esteem (or *lack* of it) affects everything you do and helps determine whether you make the most of your life. *Now* is the time to bolster your self-esteem and keep it strong.

HOW'S YOUR SELF-ESTEEM?

Here is a work sheet to help you evaluate how you think about yourself. Make a copy of this page, or write your answers on a separate sheet of paper, then evaluate them according to the key on the next page. Answer these questions again in a year to see if your attitudes have changed.

PART 1

1. What are five good things about you?

   _____ _____ _____

   _____ _____

2. What would your friends say is your best quality?

   _____

3. What would your mother or father say is your best quality?

   _____

4. Name two things you are good at:

   _____ _____

5. Name one thing you are proud of:

   _____

PART 2

Put a *T* for true or an *F* for false in front of each of these statements.

___ When my teacher praises me, I believe him or her.

___ I usually say what I mean.

___ If someone disagrees with my opinion, I still believe what I believe.

___ I basically like how I look.

___ I am happy with myself the way I am.

___ If someone compliments me, I usually respond by saying "thank you."

___ I rarely put myself down in conversations with peers.

___ I believe in my ability to make a contribution in the world.

___ If I have a goal, I give accomplishing it my best shot.

___ I believe people can change their attitudes.

WHAT YOUR ANSWERS MEAN

If you thought of positive answers to all of the questions in Part 1, this indicates that you genuinely like and respect yourself—a sign of high self-esteem. If you couldn't think of affirming answers to all the questions, you need to develop a better sense of your strengths.

For Part 2, count up your "true" answers. Here's what the total means:

1–3 "true" answers: You don't feel very confident about yourself. The next section, "Things to Do," will give you practical suggestions for improving your self-esteem.

4–6 "true" answers: Your current self-esteem level is about average, but you could certainly improve it. See the next section for details.

7–10 "true" answers: You have strong self-esteem. Read the rest of this section for tips on keeping your self-esteem level up.

—adapted from *Developing Self-Esteem: A Positive Guide for Personal Success*,
by Connie Palladino

Things to Do

LISTEN TO YOURSELF TALK

What you say can reveal a great deal about your self-esteem. Pay attention to the phrases you use. Here are indicators that your self-esteem may be low, along with ways to speak more positively.

✪ Ending statements tentatively with the phrase "you know?" This shows that you need someone to approve of what you said. Just finish the sentence and wait for a response.

✪ Putting yourself down with statements such as "I hate my thighs" or "I'm no good at this." Negative statements like these reinforce the idea that you are a bad person, which you aren't. When you catch yourself doing this, think of a positive statement to replace the put-down.

✪ Not accepting compliments. If someone says something nice about you, instead of disagreeing or downplaying the compliment by cracking a joke, say thank you. This may feel uncomfortable at first, but you'll get used to it.

✪ Saying "I don't know," even if you do. You'll make a better impression if you answer confidently.

✪ Agreeing with someone even if you don't feel the same way. Of course, you don't necessarily have to reveal your opinion, but you don't have to *agree*.

SPEAK UP!

Probably the most basic thing you can do to improve your self-esteem is to sound off on your own behalf. How do you do this without alienating people or feeling uncomfortable? According to Gershen Kaufman and Lev Raphael, authors of *Stick Up for Yourself! Every Kid's Guide to Personal Power and Positive Self-Esteem,* speaking up doesn't mean getting back at someone, acting superior, or ignoring others' feelings or opinions. It simply means stating your opinion, referring to your feelings, and asking for what you want.

Here's an example. Ana Jeronimus, thirteen, of Duluth, Minnesota, wanted to play baseball with some boys on her street. She told them she wanted to play, but they said no. She got her glove, then asked again. "One kid in particular was being mean, saying 'Geez, Ana,' as if I didn't belong there," says Jeronimus. She didn't see any reason why she shouldn't play. They offered to let her play the position of "full-time catcher," so she declined and left again. When she returned, the boy who had been mean had left, and the others apologized and said she could play. "I was glad I spoke up for myself," says Jeronimus, "because after I left, they realized they had done the wrong thing. I feel pretty confident about myself now."

You can be liked by others and still get your point across. Practice saying what's on your mind in a friendly but straightforward way. Think of the many successful women in the public eye who gracefully speak their minds—Hillary Clinton, Oprah Winfrey, Queen Latifah, Jodie Foster, Mother Teresa, and Burmese pro-democracy leader Aung San Syuu Ki, to name a few. The more you practice verbalizing your thoughts calmly but forcefully, the more natural it will become.

KEEP A JOURNAL

A journal is a book you can use to record events, feelings, ideas, and observations about your behavior, goals, and what happens in your life.

Writing in a journal helps you tune in to your thoughts and feelings and understand yourself. According to psychologist David D. Burns, author of *The Feeling Good Handbook*, "Once you get [your thoughts] down on paper, you develop a more objective perspective." This perspective will give you a chance to stand back and view yourself. It may help to clarify your opinions and feelings so that when the opportunity arises for you to voice them, you will feel more sure of yourself and your convictions. Latoya Hunter, who kept a journal when she was twelve that was later published under the title *The Diary of Latoya Hunter: My First Year in Junior High School* (Random House, 1992), found this to be true. She wrote: "I didn't know that I had so many feelings and opinions before [keeping this journal], because I never really had to sit down and write about how I feel."

Your journal can be as simple as a spiral notebook you buy at the drugstore or as elaborate as a cloth book with blank pages. You don't have to write a lot or even record something every day; just think of it as a place you can express yourself when you feel like it. Start by recording the date, then write what's on your mind.

If you're having trouble getting started, try one of these ideas:

✿   Describe a conversation you had with someone and how you felt about it.

✿   Make a list of what is important to you (for example, getting good grades, earning a lot of money, being honest, being popular, or getting along with your parents). Then write about why these things are important to you.

☆ Make a list of ten things you like about yourself.

☆ Set goals: What do you want to accomplish by the time you are fifteen, twenty, and twenty-five?

☆ Write a poem about yourself.

☆ Do a stream-of-consciousness piece—just write whatever comes into your mind.

☆ Cut out images from magazines and make a collage about yourself.

☆ Record your dreams and what they seem to mean to you.

☆ Read other girls' diaries to get ideas. Here are three good ones:

Only Opal: The Diary of a Young Girl, by Opal Whiteley, adapted by Jane Boulton (Putnam, 1994).

Zlata's Diary: A Child's Life in Sarajevo, by Zlata Filipovic (Penguin, 1994).

Anne Frank: The Diary of a Young Girl, The Definitive Edition, by Anne Frank, edited by Otto H. Frank and Mirjam Pressler (Doubleday, 1981).

DO AN EXTRACURRICULAR ACTIVITY

Extracurricular pursuits such as debating, public speaking, martial arts, or playing an instrument in a band are excellent ways to develop self-confidence and learn valuable skills. By trying out a variety of activities, you may also discover some new hobbies and interests. If any of your activities are sports, that's all the better, since when girls improve their physical strength and skills, they often feel more self-assured in general. (See chapter 9, Know the Score, for more on this subject.)

JOIN THE GIRL SCOUTS

Many girls report that being in the Girl Scouts has helped them gain self-confidence. The program focuses on developing leadership abilities, and you can practice a variety of skills, such as planning, organizing, and public speaking. Girl Scout projects vary according to local chapter, but some activities include doing beach cleanups, holding conferences, building bridges over streams, and conducting community service projects such as painting group houses for runaway kids. To find the Girl Scout chapter in your area, look under *Girl Scouts* in the white pages of the telephone book.

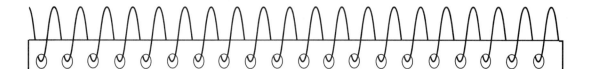

GET A MENTOR

Do you know a woman who is interested in you and your life—someone other than a family member? If you do, she could serve as a role model or mentor for you. According to Kristen Golden of the *Ms.* Foundation, having a female role model can boost a girl's confidence level. In a group of girls she interviewed, the ones who seemed the most self-confident had a "strong, confiding relationship with a woman who talked with [them] openly and listened to [them] respectfully."

If you don't currently have a mentor, you may be able to get one. The Big Brothers/Big Sisters program pairs up adult volunteer advisers with boys and girls from ages six to seventeen. You and your big sister might go to a movie, the park, or the circus, or you might just sit and talk. Look in the white pages under *Big Brothers/Big Sisters,* or contact the national organization at 230 North 13th St., Philadelphia, PA 19107; (215) 567-7000.

Finding Your Voice

by Brooke Hodess

Boston

I grew up in a male-dominated family with three older brothers, and as the only girl, it was tough making myself heard. What I had to say didn't seem very important to my brothers. I wanted to be a boy so my voice would matter. My mother knew this, and she would tell me, "If you want to be heard, fight for it." I didn't think it made sense to fight for a chance to speak in my own home, so I stayed silent most of the time. When I did express my thoughts, my brothers teased me.

However, all this changed when I went to Wheaton—an all-woman college—where I developed a strong sense of self-esteem. The message was: Believe in yourself, value your strengths, nurture your drive. I had an array of strong, outspoken female role models—not just professors, administrators, and the president, but students as well. All the student leadership roles were filled by women. I developed a sense of belonging and an activist spirit. I started to believe in myself. I began to realize that I stood for things I was willing to fight for, and I began to find my voice.

Low self-esteem made me keep quiet at the dinner table when I was growing up, but now I've made up for that. If I had known then what I know now—that my voice would have mattered if I had had faith in it—I might have spoken up more. And so I say to you: It's OK to speak up, to be outgoing, to know that you *are* important. Seek guidance from people who believe in you. Always remember who you are and where you've come from. And more than anything else, don't let anyone deny you your right to be heard.

"All serious daring starts from within."

—*Eudora Welty, writer*

Phenomenal Woman

Pretty women wonder where my secret lies.
I'm not cute or built to suit a fashion model's size
But when I start to tell them,
They think I'm telling lies.
I say,
It's in the reach of my arms,
The span of my hips,
The stride of my step,
The curl of my lips.
I'm a woman
Phenomenally.
Phenomenal woman,
That's me.

I walk into a room
Just as cool as you please,
And to a man,
The fellows stand or
Fall down on their knees.
Then they swarm around me,
A hive of honey bees.
I say,
It's the fire in my eyes,
And the flash of my teeth,
The swing in my waist,
And the joy in my feet.
I'm a woman
Phenomenally.
Phenomenal woman,
That's me.

Men themselves have wondered
What they see in me.
They try so much
But they can't touch
My inner mystery.
When I try to show them

They say they still can't see.
I say,
It's in the arch of my back,
The sun of my smile,
The ride of my breasts,
The grace of my style.
I'm a woman
Phenomenally.
Phenomenal woman,
That's me.

Now you understand
Just why my head's not bowed.
I don't shout or jump about
Or have to talk real loud.
When you see me passing
It ought to make you proud.
I say,
It's in the click of my heels,
The bend of my hair,
The palm of my hand,
The need for my care.
'Cause I'm a woman
Phenomenally.
Phenomenal woman,
That's me.

—Maya Angelou

For More Information

Choices: A Teen Woman's Journal for Self-Awareness and Personal Planning, by Mindy Bingham, Judy Edmondson, and Sandy Stryker (Advocacy Press, 1993). A workbook written to help fourteen- to twenty-year-olds with self-discovery and life decisions.

My Computer Diary, by Julie Zoellin Cramer (Stone and Associates, 1994). If you have a PC running Windows, you can use this computer program to create your own journal. It includes a calendar, a planner, and interesting information about hundreds of women. Grades five to ten. Available from the publisher, 7910 Ivanhoe Ave., Suite 319, La Jolla, CA 92037; (619) 693-6333.

Making the Most of Today: Daily Readings for Young People on Self-Awareness, Creativity, and Self-Esteem, by Pamela Espeland and Rosemary Wallner (Free Spirit, 1991). Inspirational readings to help teens handle day-to-day issues and foster personal growth.

Images, by Mattie Evans Gray. A journal for African-American girls that focuses on self-esteem and career preparation. Available from the California Department of Education, Publication Sales, P.O. Box 271, Sacramento, CA 95812; (800) 995-4099.

Girls Speak Out: Finding Your True Self, by Andrea Johnston (Scholastic, 1996). A guide written by a workshop leader to help girls ages nine to fourteen reclaim their self-esteem.

Coping Through Self-Esteem, by Rhoda McFarland (Rosen Publishing Group, 1993). Ideas to help teens accept and appreciate themselves.

The Self-Esteem and Wellness Guide for Girls, by Donna Wanner (SpiritSeeker, 1994). Written by a teacher, this book was created to help preteen and teen girls realize the benefits of self-confidence and good health.

Totally Private and Personal: Journaling Ideas for Girls and Young Women, by Jessica Wilber, (Free Spirit, 1996). The fourteen-year-old author suggests a variety of diary-keeping tips and ways to celebrate being a girl.

Building Self-Esteem Through the Museum of I: 25 Original Projects That Explore and Celebrate the Self, by Linda R. Zack (Free Spirit, 1995). Projects to help kids in grades four to eight build confidence.

Mariposa: A Workbook for Discovery and Exploration. A workbook written especially for Latina girls that features projects such as exploring cultural heritage and creating a resume. Available from Connections Leadership Project, SERVE Library, 1314 H St., Suite 200, Sacramento, CA 95814; (916) 556-1680.

Chapter 2
Go Figure

Are you satisfied with the way you look? Would you change some of your features if you could?

Most girls answer these questions by saying no, they aren't satisfied, and yes, they would change something—hip size, breast size, height, weight, skin color, nose shape. Girls tend to feel that they have to look good by conventional standards in order to be popular or even just accepted by their peers. Even *girls* judge girls based on their looks. "Girls are always so pressured to look beautiful," says Ashley Olauson, twelve, of Edina, Minnesota. "The message is that if you aren't beautiful, change yourself or be doomed to the life of a social outcast!"

That pressure is caused in large part by our cultural attitudes and how they are conveyed through the media. Women's looks are emphasized far more than men's. Turn on the TV or flip through a women's magazine, and you see images of thin, light-skinned young women with long legs, small hips, and large breasts. As prevalent as these images are, 95 percent of girls and women do not look like this—models are 9 percent taller and 23 percent thinner than the

Looks can be deceiving. The retouching of the photos of Michelle Pfeiffer featured on this foldout cover of the December 1990 issue of Esquire included cleaning up her complexion, adding color to her lips and cheeks, softening lines on her neck and around her eyes and mouth, and trimming her chin.

average woman! But if you see these kinds of images enough, you may start to think that they are the norm and that everyone should look that way.

It's difficult to be constantly bombarded by these unrealistic ideals and feel adequate by comparison. Many girls react by trying to live up to the narrowly defined standards of beauty. To alter their appearance, they exercise all the time, straighten or curl their hair, diet or fast, and some even have plastic surgery such as liposuction or nose jobs. Many become preoccupied or obsessed with their bodies, and this can lead to eating disorders such as anorexia and bulimia. One out of every five girls between ages twelve and nineteen has an eating disorder.

Knowing the difference between the world of the media and the real world can help you be more accepting of your appearance. The next time you start to feel critical of your body, look around at the girls and women you know. They come in all different shapes and sizes. Some are tall or thin, others short or stocky. Recognize that the world is made up of *real* girls and women, and that each of them is uniquely beautiful with a distinct personality that adds to her attractiveness. When you see a picture of a model, remember that the image was created, not born. The model was covered with makeup, and the photograph was selected from many taken during a photo shoot, then probably touched up with airbrushing.

Beauty News

If beauty is not defined by what you see in ads, what *is* it defined by? The truth is that beauty is subjective—people in different parts of the world have different opinions on what is attractive. According to Elaine Hatfield and Susan Sprecher, authors of *Mirror, Mirror . . . The Importance of Looks in Everyday Life,* "People in different cultures do not even agree on which features are *important,* much less what is good-looking and what is not." In Africa, for instance, large lips are considered attractive, so the girls in a certain tribe insert wooden disks in their lips to accentuate the shape. Among the Padaung women of Burma, long necks are considered beautiful, so girls wear stacks of heavy brass or iron rings as necklaces to stretch the skin and vertebrae. In addition, beauty ideals have fluctuated over time. For example, in some parts of the world centuries ago, heavy people were considered most attractive. Why? Food was scarce, and overweight people were obviously well off, while thin people were seen as malnourished and poor. The ancient Chinese believed that small female feet were superior to large feet and a sign of high class. This led to a custom (albeit cruel and painful) of binding the feet of infant girls to prevent them from growing. In the United States during the 1920s, it was fashionable to have small hips, but in the 1950s, a more voluptuous look was in style. As you can see, attractiveness is not easily or even consistently definable.

OK, you're probably thinking, *so beauty is subjective. But right now, how do I change the way I feel about my face, hair, or body?* You may not love everything about your appearance, and that's fine—neither do most people. There is nothing wrong with putting your best foot forward each day through such tactics as wearing flattering clothes or putting on makeup. Just remember that your true attractiveness does not stem from the sum of your measurements. Focus on expressing the wonderful person you are, undertaking the exciting activities you want to pursue, and experiencing what brings you joy. Ironically, once you are engaged in your life and no longer worried about how you rate according to superficial beauty standards, people will notice your inner radiance and think of you as beautiful.

Who really looks like this?

The Gardener and the Tree

Once upon a time, there was a gardener who loved small trees. He didn't like trees that were tall and full—only small and dainty ones—and he planted all varieties of them in his grove. One year he noticed a young tree coming up that he hadn't planted. Normally he grew only trees that he had carefully selected, but this tree's leaves were a nice almond shape and its trunk had a nice texture and lovely coloring, so he decided to let it stay.

The tree grew, and the gardener became unhappy because it wasn't small like the others but had a large trunk and full branches. So he decided that he would make this tree small like the others. First he chopped off its long and bushy branches and cut its trunk to a shorter height. Then he stopped giving it water as regularly as he did the other trees and built a shade around it so that it wouldn't get so much

sun. He believed that if he held back nourishment, the tree would stop growing and become small and dainty like the other trees in his grove.

Gradually the tree did stop growing, but instead of becoming a small, dainty tree, it became a large tree that never grew. Its trunk was full and ready to support many branches, but they had all been cut away. The sparse new growth it had managed to generate without proper sun and water was spindly and unhealthy.

One day when the gardener stopped by, he saw that the bark had lost its lovely coloring and the leaves had become thin and curled. The trunk that had been large and tall now looked silly at the shorter height. The gardener shook his head sadly and said, "What have I done? Instead of creating the tree I wanted, I have ruined the tree I had."

—**from *Coping with a Negative Body Image*, by Kathy Bowen-Woodward**

17

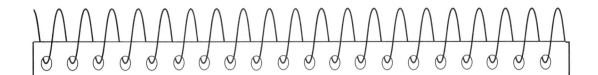

Things to Do

KEEP A BODY DIARY

You may think that if you could change one thing about the way you look, you would suddenly feel satisfied with yourself and life would be great. It's possible, but you might then find some other aspect of yourself to dislike. Psychologists say the solution is not to try to change your body, since to a large extent the way you look is genetically determined (constant aerobics can't turn a short, stocky girl into a tall, thin one). Instead, try to accept your body the way it is and get in the habit of replacing self-criticism with affirming thoughts.

One way to do this is to keep a diary to monitor how you think of your body. Every evening write down whether you felt critical of your appearance during the day. Then figure out if there were other reasons you could have been upset—people sometimes feel insecure about their bodies when they're reacting to some unrelated event. If you can determine that you were actually upset about something else, you may find that the negative feelings about your body go away. Then end the day's diary entry appreciating your body by writing something positive about it.

Dear Diary,

Today in the locker room, I looked in the mirror and said, "I hate my hips!" I look like I've already had a baby, but all the other girls in gym class have slim figures.
Then I realized that I was feeling unpopular and wondering if people like being my friend. I was afraid that people won't like me, because I'm not a cheerleader. On the positive side, I like the way my wavy hair frames my face—very flattering! I'm lucky because I'll never need a perm.

Hannah

DISCOVER YOUR BODY'S STRENGTHS

There is something more beautiful than a stereotypically beautiful body, and that's a person using her body gracefully. The sight of a soccer player using her muscular legs is inspiring, and so is that of a short, agile jockey riding her horse across the finish line, or a lanky marathon runner out in first place. Find out what your body can do. Focus on developing your strength, flexibility, and physical ability through an activity such as yoga, dance, lifting weights, or karate. (See chapter 9, Know the Score, for more ideas.) This can help you feel proud of your body and less self-conscious.

LEARN ABOUT EATING DISORDERS

You've probably heard of anorexia and bulimia, two conditions that are common among teenage girls. With anorexia, a person undergoes serious weight loss, falling below her normal body weight, through dieting and excessive exercise. Bulimia is characterized by bouts of bingeing (eating large amounts of food), followed by purging (getting rid of the food by vomiting or using laxatives). These conditions disrupt a girl's normal body functioning and can endanger her health. For example, bulimia causes the production of excess stomach acids, and the weight loss associated with anorexia can decrease muscle tone, cause osteoporosis, and in some extreme cases, result in death. For instance, Christy Henrich, one of the best gymnasts in the U.S., died from anorexia in 1994.

Eating disorders are generally considered to be caused by psychological and emotional factors. A girl may use food to comfort herself or avoid feeling unresolved feelings. She may unconsciously adopt unhealthy eating patterns if she feels that part of her life is out of control, because it gives her a way to control *something.* She may also develop an eating disorder as a way to unconsciously avoid some type of pressure in her life (which could have originated in the past). These are just a few possibilities. You can find out more about eating disorders by reading the books listed on page 22.

If you think you may have a problem with food, don't despair, as eating disorders are treatable and you are certainly not alone. It's important that you talk to someone such as a school counselor, your family doctor, or another adult you trust. If you have a friend who's exhibiting symptoms of an eating disorder, let her know you're concerned. Don't judge her eating habits, as this will only make her feel more anxious. Suggest that she talk to someone who can help, and offer to go with her.

COMPARE IMAGES THEN AND NOW

The definition of what is beautiful has changed throughout history. Want proof? Get a friend and go to the library. Look at magazines or books from two separate decades that are at least one decade apart (the 1920s and the 1950s, for example). Make copies of five of your favorite images from each decade, then lay them next to similar images from recent magazines and books. Look at figure shape and weight (voluptuous and heavy? pencil-thin?), height, hair style, breast size, amount of makeup, and what the model is doing to make her appear more beautiful. Also notice changes in fashion, as styles were meant to emphasize the popular beauty ideals of the time. What are your conclusions?

PROTEST A PAGEANT

Beauty pageants, with their emphasis on the way contestants look in bathing suits and evening gowns, convey the message that women are valued primarily for their looks, not for who they are or what they accomplish. But thanks to protests by women and

girls, some pageants (such as small-town contests) are attracting fewer contestants and getting fewer sponsors. Former model Ann Simonton is known for her protests of the Miss California pageant. She helped create "Myth California" counterpageants outside the actual pageants and used creative and funny tactics to make her messages stick. Once, when she wore a thirty-pound evening dress made entirely of bologna, she was mistaken as a contestant. Another year, she wore a bathing suit made of raw steak and a pageant-style "Miss Steak" banner to make the point that pageants treat women like pieces of meat.

If you want to help a pageant go out of style, start on a small scale. To find out when a qualifying pageant is being held in your area, call the Miss America (609/345-7571), Miss Teen USA, Miss USA, or Miss Universe (310/553-2555) pageant. If your city sponsors a hometown pageant, write a letter to the editor of your local newspaper expressing your opinion.

Next step: Protest a pageant. Any citizen has the right to picket and distribute information as long as you don't block entries or exits and you're not on private property (city streets and sidewalks are public property). Don't protest alone—invite friends to help you make signs and hand out flyers. You can also start a dialogue about pageants at school. The whole point is to educate people who might not be aware of pageants' negative effects on women. For other ideas or inspiration, contact Ann Simonton at Media Watch, P.O. Box 618, Santa Cruz, CA, 95061; (408) 423-6355; mwatch@cruzio.com.

The Power of Muscles

by Gloria Steinem

New York

Rick Bard

I come from a generation of women who didn't do sports. Being a cheerleader or a drum majorette was as far as our imaginations or role models could take us. Oh yes, there was also being a strutter—one of a group of girls who marched and danced and turned cartwheels in front of the high school band at football games. Did you know that big football universities actually gave strutting scholarships? That shouldn't sound any more bizarre than football scholarships, yet somehow it does.

But even winning one of those rare positions, the stuff that dreams were made of, was more about body display than about the considerable skill they required. You could forget about trying out for them if you didn't have the right face and figure, and my high school was full of girls who had learned to do back flips and twirl flaming batons, all to no avail. Winning wasn't about being the best in an objective competition or achieving a personal best, or even about becoming healthy or fit. It was about *being chosen.*

That's one reason I and other women of my generation grew up believing—as many girls still do—that the most important thing about a female body is not what it does but how it looks, and that a woman should not be strong.

However, I gradually became aware of the benefits of being strong. Several of my unathletic friends had deserted me by joining gyms, becoming joggers, or discovering the pleasure of learning to yell and kick in self-defense class. Others who had young daughters described the unexpected thrill of seeing them learn to throw a ball or run with a freedom that hadn't been part of our lives in conscious memory.

The female ideal remains weak unless we organize to change it. The suffragists shed the unhealthy corsets that produced such a tiny-waisted, big-breasted look that fainting and smelling salts became routine. Instead, they brought in bloomers and bicycling. The point is: When women rebel against patriarchal standards, female muscle becomes more accepted.

I've come to believe that society's acceptance of muscular women may be one of the most important measures of change. Yes, we need progress everywhere, but an increase in our physical strength could have more impact on the everyday lives of most women than the occasional role model in the boardroom or in the White House. Each of us must have our own strength.

....

Gloria Steinem is one of the most celebrated leaders of the women's movement and a cofounder of **Ms.** *magazine.*

"I much prefer brains to curves in women. Honesty, courage, and a sensible outlook are traits I find appealing."

—*Ted Danson, actor*

For More Information

Food Fight: A Guide to Eating Disorders for Pre-Teens and Their Parents, by Janet Bode (Simon & Schuster, 1997). Offers practical suggestions for helping individuals regain control of their eating habits.

Real Gorgeous: The Truth about Body & Beauty, by Kaz Cooke (Norton, 1995). A humorous book written to help girls and women gain perspective on our beauty-obsessed culture.

When Food's a Foe: How to Confront and Conquer Eating Disorders, by Nancy J. Kolodny (Little, Brown, rev. ed. 1992). Tells how to recognize symptoms that may signal an eating disorder and how to get help.

The Beauty Trap, by Elaine Landau (New Discovery Books, 1994). Examines society's attitudes toward beauty and the ways women and girls are affected. Grades seven to ten.

Weight: A Teenage Concern, by Elaine Landau (Lodestar Books, 1991). Teen reflections on being overweight combined with techniques for controlling weight and accepting your body shape.

Straight Talk about Eating Disorders, by Michael Maloney and Rachel Kranz (Dell, 1993). Explores cultural attitudes about weight and food, and provides guidelines for identifying eating disorders.

Safe Dieting for Teens, by Linda Ojeda (Hunter House, 1993). Presents a healthful alternative to fad dieting and weight-loss centers.

Eating Disorders Awareness and Prevention Inc., 603 Stewart St., Suite 803, Seattle, WA 98101; (206) 382-3587. Has brochures and educational materials.

National Association of Anorexia Nervosa and Associated Disorders, Box 7, Highland Park, IL 60035; (847) 831-3438. Offers free services, including referrals to counselors and self-help groups.

Chapter 3
You Go, Girl!

Picture a teacher or parent telling a twelve-year-old girl to calm down, talk more softly, or stop clowning around. Now picture the same scenario, but with a boy. Which is more likely to happen?

In our culture, boys are allowed—even encouraged—to be rambunctious (after all, "Boys will be boys"), while girls who show the same level of enthusiasm are often reprimanded. Boys learn to feel comfortable being the center of attention, whereas girls learn not to draw attention to themselves. As a result of this subtle pressure, many girls start out as spontaneous and free-spirited but gradually rein in their happy, silly, "wild" selves, control their behavior, laugh less, and become more "ladylike." Is this true for you? If your parents are putting pressure on you to quit being a tomboy, you may be becoming less adventurous. If your friends are focusing on their appearance, you may be spending less time doing what you enjoy and instead focusing on your looks, too. Or you may just naturally be feeling more self-conscious and fearing that you'll offend others by being too outspoken or loud.

Laurel King, author of *A Whistling Woman Is Up to No Good: Finding Your Wild Woman*, says the phenomenon of girls conforming to our culture's expectations is with us today because society has always tried to keep women "tamed." She points out that it used to be considered inappropriate for a woman to so much as whistle. Those women who dared to whistle were obviously not inhibited or afraid to be noticed, and they were considered a threat to society. In fact, women were burned at the stake for it! Even in the early twentieth century, female whistling was still considered "unlady-like."

Women and girls can whistle all they want now, but may still not feel OK just being themselves. This chapter is meant to help you keep your natural self intact, to

Climbing Lessons

by Andrea Floyd, fourteen

Sebastopol, California

A lot of people don't understand rock climbing. I used to be one of them. Like the average person, I cringed at the thought of hanging by my fingertips on a steep rock face with nothing between me and the ground except air. I felt that it was a boring thing guys do to try to prove they're macho. The guys I knew wore a strange-looking harness with a rope attached to it, jammed their hands and feet into a bunch of little pockets in a rock, and called it fun!

Once I tried climbing, however, everything changed. For one thing, I learned a valuable lesson: You shouldn't prejudge people or activities, because you can miss out on some pretty amazing experiences. I also learned that some women have become very well known as professional climbers, and I learned that girls can climb just as well as guys.

I set out to climb my first rock with my brother when I was thirteen. People thought I was kind of crazy, and I felt like I was doing something daring. I was intimidated by the prospect of ever getting up that wall, but I overcame the fear and kept at it. Toward the end of the summer, my dad, brother, and I went on a climbing trip to the eastern Sierras, which are beautiful mountains. It was here that I knew climbing was for me.

Climbing is both challenging and relaxing. When you're thirty feet up, you're forced to think about getting to the top, not about the stress of school and everyday life. It is physically and mentally rewarding. Most important, it has affected my life in positive ways—giving me a new sense of confidence and respect for myself. I'm glad I took a chance on it, and I know that it will continue to be one of my passions and a source of inspiration for me for many years to come.

remember to laugh, to let your soul shine. If you can do this, you'll be better adjusted later in your life. And life can be much more rewarding if you learn to really *live*.

So if you feel like whistling, go right ahead. Sing, laugh, yell, dance, talk, have a pillow fight…do whatever expresses you best in any given moment. Make a concerted effort to take a few risks every week, doing things such as trying out for the school play or going on a backpacking trip. In short, go for it!

A Funny Story

by Roz Warren

Bala Cynwyd, Pennsylvania

If you're the kind of girl who likes to goof around, crack jokes, or make fun of things, you're doing something right. Humor is very powerful stuff. Everybody loves to laugh, and if you can make others laugh, that makes you valuable to them.

Sometimes people—particularly guys—find funny girls threatening. They're probably scared that if you have a sharp wit, you could end up turning it on *them*. Maybe that's why our culture gives girls the message that it's "unfeminine" to crack jokes and laugh. When a boy says a girl has a good sense of humor, sometimes what he really means is that she laughs at his jokes (whether they're funny or not), not that *her* jokes make him laugh.

But being able to laugh and make fun of things that deserve to be mocked is one of the best things you can do. Not only is it fun, but being able to laugh makes you stronger. I'm not saying that you've got to run around grinning all the time. Sometimes it's difficult to find anything to laugh about. But if you can manage not to lose your sense of humor, it can help you get through rough times. Laughter is a real survival mechanism. Don't let anyone talk you out of it!

Roz Warren edits and publishes humor books for women. Her works include **The Best Contemporary Women's Humor** *and* **Revolutionary Laughter.**

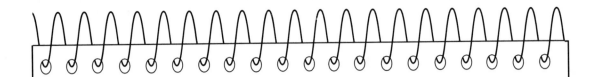

Things to Do

CHECK YOURSELF OUT

Pay attention to the way you behave around different people and groups of people. Are you less talkative around boys? Sillier around your best friend? More serious around your family? Without even knowing it, you could be modifying the way you act in different situations. Again, a certain amount of difference is natural. But if you find that you're being less spontaneous or carefree than you used to be, that's something to think about, because you don't have to behave in any certain way to be liked. Ask a good friend to let you know when she thinks your behavior changes—for better or worse. This will help you recognize your behavior patterns and change them.

GO ON AN ADVENTURE

Have you ever wanted to strike out on your own or just do something a little bit bold . . . but squelched the urge because you were worried that it would be too difficult or people wouldn't approve? Well, guess what? Challenges can be exciting, and does it really matter if some people don't support you for doing something a little out of the ordinary? Plus, once you've embarked on your activity, you'll find others who share your enthusiasm.

One way to make an adventure easier is to get a bunch of girls to do it together so you'll feel safer and less intimidated than you might if you did it alone. Challenging outdoor activities are one way for a group of girls to "get wild." If the idea of doing something like rock climbing, sailing, or backpacking sounds good to you, talk to your parents about it. There may be an outdoor adventure program in your area that welcomes teens. Call Outward Bound (see page 28 for the number) to see if there are any teen adventure programs near you.

CELEBRATE UNINHIBITED WOMEN

History books may give you the idea that women throughout the ages were soft-spoken and blended into the background, but that's simply not true. Writers have started to spread the word about some of these important women so you can find out about what they really did (see page 28 for a few sources). Read about Dorothy Parker or Mother Jones, or do a report on Annie Oakley. Go see contemporary women comedians, musicians, performers, and speakers whenever you can. Watch videos featuring Lily Tomlin, Gilda Radner, or Xena. These are just a few ways to get started.

We do something dumb,
completely ridiculous,
we laugh hysterically for
    20 minutes.
People who are not included
involved think we are crazy,
immature, obnoxious.
It's hard for them to understand
the fun we have when
we're with each other

because they're our own games,
    our own group.
We can also be serious.
They sometimes can't understand
    our problems.
Why are we so upset about coming in
    at 10 o'clock.
We are good support for each other.
Just having your friends near
makes everything easier.

**—A poem by teenager Cecelia
Manley, from *Almost Grown***

**"One can never consent to creep when one feels an impulse to
soar."**

—Helen Keller, activist

Name: Annie Edson Taylor

First female to: plummet over Niagara Falls in a barrel

Preceding events: A teacher in Michigan, Taylor needed money to pay the mortgage on her farm, so she came up with this daredevil publicity stunt. Hoping that proceeds from a paying audience would make her rich, she braved the drop over Horseshoe Falls in 1901. She survived the ordeal but was in no mood to celebrate, as her manager kept most of the money.

For More Information

Buffalo Gals: Women of the Old West, by Brandon M. Miller (Lerner Publications, 1995). Available from the publisher at (800) 328-4929.

Dreams into Deeds: Nine Women Who Dared, by Linda Peavy and Ursula Smith (Scribner's, 1985). Biographies of nine remarkable women.

"Women Who Dared" postcards, published by Pomegranate Artbooks, feature women who have dared to take on exciting challenges. To order, contact the National Women's History Project, 7738 Bell Rd., Windsor, CA 95492-8518; (707) 838-6000.

Outward Bound, National Office, Route 9D R2, Box 280, Garrison, NY 10524; (800) 243-8520. Hosts coed and female-only outdoor adventure programs that help participants become more aware of themselves and their environment. Age fourteen and up.

Chapter 4
Good Housekeeping

How do you learn what it means to be female?

You don't go to the store and get a book about it, or learn about it at school. You get it from your biggest role models: your parents. In many homes, for example, the mother is the one who does all the cooking, because her mother did it, and on back through the generations. If you see your mother doing most or all of the cooking, you might assume that mothers are supposed to cook. (Of course, some women prefer to always do the cooking, and that's fine if it's their choice.) If your father or another man does the yard work, you might get the idea that it's "men's work," even though you or your mother could do it just as easily. If the boys in your family have more privileges than the girls, such as later curfews or being able to watch more TV, you may get the message that boys are allowed more freedom.

The men and boys in your family can also affect your attitudes about femaleness. They may be supportive of women's rights or make fun of you for being a "women's libber." If they are sympathetic, they can help you feel confident in the belief that you deserve to be treated equally. And if they aren't supportive, that's OK, too, because interacting with them can make you a stronger person. All of this means that your family can be a good place for exploring your beliefs about womanhood, experimenting with less traditional roles for yourself, and getting real-life experience standing up for your beliefs.

"Women's Work"

Almost since the beginning of time, women have traditionally been in charge of household maintenance and child care. They still do the majority of the housework in every country in the world. The United States has one of the better records, but it's not much better. Up until the 1970s, it was standard for American women to do more housework because most wives stayed home and their husbands had jobs. Now the majority of women work outside the home, either because their incomes are needed to support their families or because, like most men, they prefer to have a career and be financially independent.

Here's where it gets unbalanced: Even when women work full-time outside the home, many still automatically fall into the role of housekeeper, particularly if their mothers did most of the chores. It's as if women work another workday after their shift at the office, says author Arlie Hochschild in her groundbreaking book *The Second Shift*. Girls also take on more responsibility for housework than boys do. According to a study done at Arizona State University, in homes where both parents worked, teen girls did an average of ten hours of chores a week—three times as much as their brothers did.

Tradition can be tough to change, but in a family with two working parents, housework should ideally be shared equally between the parents, as well as between the sons and daughters. This is easier said than done because men and boys are conditioned by society that they shouldn't have to do housework, and many of them are good at getting out of it (for instance, by "forgetting" to do chores, acting like they don't know how, or doing a bad job so they won't be asked again). Some men and boys point out that outdoor work, such as changing the oil in the car and mowing the lawn, qualifies as housework. But there is usually much less outdoor work—which can be done at someone's convenience—than there are scheduled daily chores such as meal preparation and washing dishes.

Your home is a good place to start examining the stereotypical roles that women and men adopt. Ask for what you want and what's fair! Start by encouraging sharing of household jobs, and ask your parents to support other types of equality around the house, such as establishing the same curfews and privileges for the boys and the girls. If every girl expects and encourages her family members to be fair, the status quo will change.

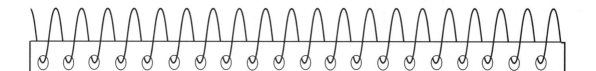

Things to Do

DIVIDE UP THE HOUSEWORK

Does your brother leave the house every time your parents ask for help cleaning up? If you think the housework isn't evenly distributed in your family, talk to your parents. Ask them to have a family meeting and assign everyone certain tasks. For reference, they can make a handy chart with everyone's responsibilities so that everyone knows what's expected. Here's how to make a chart:

1. List all the household duties.

2. Give each chore a point value from 1 to 4 based on how much time and involvement it requires (1 is an easy task; 4 is a big deal).

3. Look at the sample chart below and draw a chart for your household.

4. For the upcoming week, divide the chores so that the point values basically add up equally. Put each person's duties in a separate column.

5. Put the list on the refrigerator so everyone can see what their jobs are that week.

6. The next week, rotate the sets of chores. Note: If someone prefers a particular chore (for example, if you love to mow the lawn), schedule that chore for that person more often, as long as everyone else doesn't mind. The point is to make sure everyone has the same amount of work, and no one is stuck with the same job if they don't want it. This system should spread the responsibility more even
   and make it harder for people to avoid doing their share without feeling pressure from the rest of the family. And even if the chart only calls attention to the fact that some people are not pulling their weight, that's progress!

CHORES
July 18–26

Mom
Cooking, weeknights (4)
Grocery shopping (1)

Dad
Mowing lawn (2)
Cooking, weekend (3)

Sarah
Dishes, weeknights (3)
Taking out trash (2)

Jeremy
Dishes, weekends (2)
Laundry (3)

Marc
Feeding, walking dog every day (3)
Dusting (1)
Vacuuming (1)

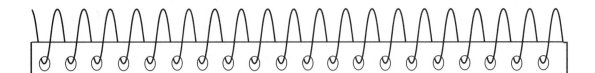

HELP A MAN DO CHORES

One way to experiment with roles is to do projects or chores that your father, stepfather, uncle, older brother, or some other male usually does. Depending on your family and where you live (in a house or an apartment), this could mean fixing or varnishing furniture, replacing light fixtures and lightbulbs, troubleshooting computer problems, hooking up stereo speakers, fixing a blown fuse, mowing the lawn, working on the car, cleaning the garage or basement, painting a fence, landscaping, or raking leaves. Guys are encouraged to try to fix things, and girls often come to depend on their help (this is called learned helplessness), but it's important for you to know how to fix things yourself so you become resourceful and independent. And later on, you'll be a good role model for your own daughters if you have them.

"Outdoor work can be fun, and it's not just boys' work," says John Moline of Duluth, Minnesota, the father of three boys and one girl, twelve-year-old Jill. He and Jill recently scraped and painted the fence around their yard. Not all the projects with her dad have been easy, but Jill says that having a good attitude has helped. "Something might seem hard at first, but not after you start doing it," she says. And I like having time to share with my father."

TRADE PLACES WITH YOUR BROTHER

Many girls have brothers who don't understand or support women's rights ("Isn't everyone equal already?"). Don't despair—perhaps you can open his eyes a little. For

one day (preferably on a weekend), ask him to "trade identities" with you so he can see what life is like for a girl (and you can see what it's like to be male). Ask him to do what you do all day. Alert your parents to the experiment so they can treat each of you as the opposite sex. Of course, you'll have to be yourselves for certain things, but try to get into the act. At the end of the day, get together and talk about what you experienced. He will probably gain a new sense of appreciation for what it means to be female, and you could learn a few things, too.

If he still doesn't see things differently, that's all right. Remember: What's most important is that you stick to your beliefs, whether or not he converts! It may be hard for him to admit that you have a point, but in time he may come to respect your views and even agree with you. Many boys who grow up with independent-minded sisters feel that it affects their adult lives in a good way. "I'm glad I had sisters who support women's rights," says Ryan Stanley, twenty-seven, of Palo Alto, California. "They helped me understand sexism and what girls and women have to deal with, and it has helped me in my relationships with women."

MAKE A FEMALE FAMILY TREE

Have you ever traced your family roots? This process can help you see what other women in your family have done with their lives, as well as give you a new sense of personal awareness and self-esteem. "People generally trace their ancestry through the male lineage," says Jan Stoltman, coordinator of a program for girls called the Mentor Project. "When they discover what the women in their family have done, they are totally amazed."

Try to find out what kind of people the women in your family were, what was important to them, and what struggles they faced. Ask your parents to tell you whatever they know, and take notes. Did your parents or other relatives save any journals or letters they wrote? These can be invaluable sources of details.

Once you've pulled together all the information, make a family-tree diagram. If you can, include copies of photographs of your great-grandmother, grandmother, mother, yourself, and your sisters if you have any. Then write a brief history of each of the women. Notice if there were or are any common life achievements, activities, or beliefs among the women. Then write a paragraph about any common threads you have identified. If you don't have enough information to discern common areas, don't worry about it—even just researching individual ancestors' backgrounds will help. "Once you discover the voices and actions of the women in your family, you are reminded that you are connected to a lineage," says Stoltman. "It is very liberating. . . . You can carry that power forward."

★★★ GOOD NEWS ★★★

While equal sharing of housework by men and women seems a way off, things have been improving, according to John Robinson, professor of sociology at the University of Maryland. His figures show that in 1965, American men did 15 percent of the housework, and that twenty years later, in 1985, they did 33 percent. In addition, a study by *New Woman* magazine found that since the 1970s, men have increasingly felt pressure to do housework.

Housework

You know, there are times
    when we happen to be
just sitting there quietly
    watching TV,
when the program we're watching
    will stop for a while
and suddenly someone
    appears with a smile
and starts to show us
    how terribly urgent
it is to buy some brand
    of detergent
        or soap
        or cleanser
        or cleaner
        or powder
        or paste
        or wax
        or bleach—
to help with the housework.

Now, most of the time
    it's a lady we see
who's doing the housework
    on TV.
She's cheerfully scouring
    a skillet or two,
or she's polishing pots
    'til they gleam like new,
or she's scrubbing the tub,
    or she's mopping the floors,
or she's wiping the stains
    from the walls and the doors,
or she's washing the windows,
    the dishes, the clothes,
or cleaning the "fridge,"
    or the stove or the sink
with a lighthearted smile
    and a friendly wink
and she's doing her best

to make us think
that *her* soap
    (or detergent
    or cleanser
    or cleaner
    or powder
    or paste
    or wax
    or bleach)
is the best one
that there is in the whole wide world!

And maybe it is . . .
and maybe it isn't . . .
and maybe it does what they
    say it will do . . .
but I'll tell you one thing
    I *know* is true:

The lady we see
    when we're watching TV—
the lady who smiles
    as she scours
        or scrubs
        or rubs
        or washes
        or wipes
        or mops
        or dusts
        or cleans—
or whatever she does
on our TV screens—
that lady is smiling because she's an
    actress.
And she's earning money
for learning those speeches
that mention those wonderful
    soaps
      and detergents
      and cleansers

and cleaners
and powders
and pastes
and waxes
and bleaches.
So the very next time
    you happen to be
just sitting there quietly
    watching TV,
and you see some nice lady
    who smiles as
she scours
        or scrubs
        or rubs
        or washes
        or wipes
        or mops
        or dusts
        or cleans
    remember:
Nobody smiles doing housework
but those ladies you see on TV.
Because even if
the soap

or detergent
or cleanser
or cleaner
or powder
or paste
or wax
or bleach
that you use
    is the very best one—
housework
    is just no fun.

Children,
when you have a house of your own
make sure, when there's housework to do,
that you don't have to do it alone.
Little boys, little girls,
when you're big husbands and wives,
if you want all the days of your lives
to seem sunny as summer weather
make sure, when there's housework to do,
that you do it together.

—Sheldon Harnick

My Brother Does Dishes

by Brazley Daraja, thirteen

Hempstead, New York

At my house we have a system for doing housework. Mom tries to keep it equally divided, and I think it's pretty fair. For dishes, I do them one week, my brother does them the next week, and my mom the third week. When someone is doing the dishes, the other is taking out the garbage. If I clean the living room, my brother cleans the bathroom.

I'm glad we have it organized this way. At some of my friends' houses, the girls do the dishes and their brothers don't. The boys do the "boy stuff," like taking out the garbage and washing the car. That's not fair, because cleaning the house is hard. Taking out a bag of garbage a day is nothing compared to doing the dishes from breakfast, lunch, and dinner. Washing the car every now and then is easy!

It wasn't always this way at my house. My brother used to say he didn't have to do the dishes because he's a boy. My mom would tell him that men aren't better than women, and then he would have to do them for another week! I don't know where he got it, but he had this idea that women belong in the kitchen. He said when he grows up, he's going to wear the pants in the family and his wife is going to stay home with the children. I told him I thought he'd been watching too much Al Bundy. So we started fighting. He pushed me, but I just beat him up because I'm stronger.

Now that he's ten and I'm thirteen, we don't argue as much anymore (his punches hurt now!) and we're able to talk about problems. My mom and I got those chauvinistic ideas out of his head. Now he'll even volunteer to do the dishes. If it's my turn to do them and I want to go to the mall, he'll say he'll do them for me. Once I asked him, "Do I have to pay you back?" And he said no.

He really believes that it's a good thing to share the housework and to be equal in other ways. For example, once he and I were at my friend's house. In response to a question from my friend, her mom said, "You know you have to ask your father about that because he's the boss." My brother asked, "How come? Why aren't you in charge? What makes him better?" My friend's mom just looked at me. I was surprised and embarrassed. But afterward I told my brother I was glad he said it. We need more boys like him in the world!

"When I was ten, I was told somebody's got to clean the fish. Well, my idea of feminism is that everyone cleans the fish."

—Cyndi Lauper, singer

For More Information

All About You: An Adventure of Self-Discovery, by Aylette Jenness (New Press, 1994). Helps you develop awareness about your family background, gender, identity, ethnicity, and culture.

The Great Ancestor Hunt: The Fun of Finding Out Who You Are, by Lila Perl (Houghton Mifflin, 1990). A handbook for delving into your roots for grades four to eight.

Free to Be . . . A Family: A Book about All Kinds of Belonging, by Marlo Thomas and Friends (Bantam, 1987). A kids' book of stories and songs about what it means to be part of a family and be yourself at the same time.

How to Tape Instant Oral Biographies, by William Zimmerman (Guarionex Press, 1994). A guide to taping life stories.

Chapter 5

Take That!

Most of the men and boys in your life are probably kind, caring, and gentle. But unfortunately, not all males are. Some take out their anger and frustrations on women, abusing them verbally, emotionally, physically, or sexually. In addition, certain aspects of our culture—rock videos, rap music lyrics, movies, and advertising—send the message that it's OK to demean and control women, and this doesn't help matters.

The good news is that our society is becoming more aware of the problem and taking steps to address it. For example, in 1994, Congress passed a law called the Violence Against Women Act, which helps fight family violence and sexual assault through various provisions.

The more women and girls acknowledge and talk about women being mistreated, the more headway we'll make. Meanwhile, the best thing you can do is to know how to look out for yourself in a potentially violent or abusive situation. It pays to be prepared—mentally and physically—just in case.

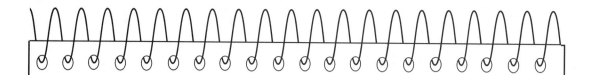

Things to Do

BE DATE SAFE

When you go on a date with a guy, your own safety is probably the furthest thing from your mind. You're probably more concerned about what you'll wear, what you'll say, and how the two of you will get along. And besides, a date is supposed to be fun! You can have a good time and still look out for yourself. Here are a few safe-dating tips:

double-date—it's safe.

☆ When you first go out with someone, you may want to double-date as a safety precaution. Your date may be completely trustworthy, but you can discover that as you get to know each other.

☆ Observe your date's behavior. How does he treat you, and how does he talk about girls or women in general? If he doesn't listen to you, or seems angry at women or talks about them in a degrading way, he may have deeper problems.

☆ Use your intuition. Many women who have been assaulted report afterward that they heard a little voice inside telling them not to get in the car with someone or agree to a date. Don't ignore those warning signals! It's always better to err on the side of safety.

☆ Don't put up with a boyfriend who doesn't treat you right. No matter how much you want to be with someone, your well-being should always come first. If you feel verbally, emotionally, or physically threatened, it's time to get out of the relationship.

The single most constructive thing you can do to ensure your personal safety is to learn self-defense. According to a 1994 U.S. government study, 61 percent of assault survivors said that resisting the attack had increased their odds of surviving. (Do note that sometimes it's best not to fight, such as when the assailant has a gun.) If you take a class, you'll learn how you can decrease your chances of being assaulted and fight off possible attacks through fairly simple physical techniques, such as using your legs and hips. You'll learn where your strengths are (boys and men may have more upper-body strength, but girls and women have an incredible amount of strength in their legs and hips). Perhaps most important, a self-defense class will boost your self-confidence, help you realize how strong you are, and help you develop a "take-charge" attitude. "Girls and women are socialized to put others first—a setup for victimization," says Helen Grieco, a self-defense teacher and National Organization for Women (NOW) activist in San Francisco. "We're taught that we aren't capable of hurting another human being, but that's a myth. Taking self-defense and learning that you're worth defending—that it's possible to have a plan of action—can positively transform your life."

Many communities offer "street safety" self-defense courses and some have classes just for teen girls. You might also want to consider taking a martial arts class such as karate or tae kwan do. Look in the yellow pages under *Women's Organizations* or *Martial Arts*.

SPREAD THE WORD ON SEXUAL ASSAULT

One reason sexual violence is so prevalent is that people rarely talk about it. "This silence creates a social atmosphere that denies the problem and isolates victims," according to the King County Sexual Assault Resource Center in Renton, Washington. To stop sexual violence, women and girls must speak out against it. Some ways to do this include: talking about the issue with friends and relatives if it feels comfortable; pointing out violence-related jokes, stereotypes, and advertisements that put down women or make them look victimized; being aware of possible incest and helping the victim stop the abuse and seek counseling; and inviting a personal-safety expert to speak about sexual assault at your school, church, or community group. If you'd like to find a speaker, start by calling your local police department and asking if an officer is assigned to speak to groups on this topic. If not, ask for a referral to another group, such as a local sexual-assault crisis center.

How I Fought Back

by Danial Dunlap, seventeen

San Francisco

I got interested in taking self-defense in 1994, when this guy had a "fatal attraction" to me. I was being stalked—he was following me to work and home, and I was afraid. Then he got a young woman to follow me, maybe because he knew I wouldn't be as cautious with her. She approached me one night when I was walking home, and when I was a block from my house, she said, "This is from [his name]," and hit me in the face with a wrench.

I heard about a self-defense class from a woman who taught classes nearby, and I signed up. The teacher taught it with a male partner who dressed up in protective padding so we could practice hitting and kicking him. I learned to be more aware of my surroundings when I'm out in public and to recognize the signs that someone is dangerous or could want to hurt me. I learned how to do heel palms, back kicks, knee kicks, eye gouging, scratching, elbow throws, and ground fighting. I learned how to shake free when somebody grabs you from behind, to scream in their ear, and to get someone off of me if I'm pinned down. We also practiced the scenario of responding to an attacker who has a knife.

I also learned that just because guys are strong, they won't necessarily have the upper hand. Guys may be heavier and stronger than girls, but I learned that girls can do certain techniques to knock them out and get them down so they can get away. I hadn't realized some basic things could be defensive moves, like stepping on someone's foot. I knew it would hurt, but I learned that if you step on it a certain way, you can disable the attacker.

You know how you see a crazy person on the street and you move faster and cross the street to get away? When I see someone like that now, I walk past without being afraid. I feel I can successfully defend myself against anybody who threatens me. This has changed my whole attitude about myself and given me a new sense of power and confidence. I recommend that every girl take self-defense!

"Woman must not depend upon the protection of man, but must be taught to protect herself."

—Susan B. Anthony

Young women practice fighting off an attacker in a Model Mugging class.

Get a Grip

It's important to know that you can defend yourself physically. But it's also helpful to be mentally prepared—to think about how you would defend yourself before you're ever in a situation where you might have to fight back. Helen Benedict, author of Safe, Strong & Streetwise, suggests these "mental self-defense" tips:

✪ Believe in your own power and strength. You are probably much stronger and faster than you think (as you'll discover if you take a self-defense class).

✪ Try to picture how you would respond if someone tried to assault you. What are your physical strengths? If you have a strong voice, it might be smart to yell. If you have strong legs, kicking or stomping on the attacker's feet might be a good strategy.

✪ If you find yourself in a situation that makes you feel scared, ask yourself what's making you feel that way. Is there anything you can do that would make you feel more secure?

✪ If you are attacked, try to keep calm and stay alert, being on the look-out for ways to escape.

✪ Trust your instincts.

For More Information

Safe, Strong & Streetwise: Sexual Safety at Home, on the Street, on Dates, on the Job, at Parties & More, by Helen Benedict (Little, Brown, 1987). Discusses physical and non-physical self-defense techniques and what to do if you're assaulted.

The Get Prepared Library of Violence Prevention for Young Women, by Donna Chaiet (Rosen Publishing Group, 1995). A series of books that provide easy techniques for staying safe in various situations. Titles include *Staying Safe on Dates, Staying Safe at School,* and *Staying Safe at Work.*

In Love & in Danger: A Teen's Guide to Breaking Free of Abusive Relationships, by Barrie Levy (Seal Press, 1992). A handbook on dating abuse.

Coping with Date Rape & Acquaintance Rape, by Andrea Parrot (Rosen Publishing Group, 1993). A comprehensive guide to rape for teens.

"Sexual Violence: What All Teens Should Know," Bureau for At-Risk Youth, 135 Dupont St., Plainview, NY 11083; (800) 999-6884. This brochure tells you how to get help if you are sexually assaulted.

"Top Secret: Sexual Assault Information for Teenagers Only," King County Sexual Assault Resource Center, P.O. Box 300, Renton, WA 98057; (206) 226-5062. Teens' stories about being assaulted, questions and answers, and safety tips. The center also has other publications.

Model Mugging, Resources for Personal Empowerment, P.O. Box 1241, Pearl River, NY 10965; (212) 650-9546. Teaches simple, effective self-defense skills in major cities throughout the country.

At School

Chapter 6
Class Acts

School's in session! You've got a schedule to follow, friends to see, a math test to take, history class to stay awake in after lunch. And if you're like many girls, unfortunately you may also have sex discrimination to face, from the people and books that are supposed to help you learn.

Teachers

Your teachers—both male and female—can be terrific influences in your life. They can inspire you, encourage you to speak up in class, and make girls realize that what they say is important. Teachers can help you feel good about yourself and confident about your future.

But teachers can also do the opposite: discourage you, ignore you during class discussions, and make you feel that you and other girls can't make meaningful contributions to the class. Why would a teacher do this? It could be because he or she categorizes people according to traditional sex roles, maybe without even realizing it. For example, your teacher may have the outdated belief that boys need to do well at school so they can get good jobs and support families but girls don't need to do well because they will become homemakers. The teacher may know things have changed but still retain old attitudes.

When a teacher doesn't treat girls and boys the same way, girls get the message that they aren't as important. He or she may do something subtle, such as choosing all boys for a fun experiment, or something really blatant, such as belittling the accomplishments of women in history. When she was a girl, Peggy Orenstein, author of a book called *Schoolgirls,* had a junior-high math book written by three people: two men and a woman named Mary P. Dolciani. "Whenever there was a typo or a problem that didn't work out right, my teacher would say, 'Mary P. must've written that problem,'" says Orenstein. Another example: "I had a teacher who let the guys get away with anything," says Andrea Johnson, fourteen, of Bradenton, Florida. "Once we were taking a

test, and the boys, clustered on one side of the room, were cheating, but the teacher didn't do anything."

Studies show that teachers commonly pay less attention to girls and praise them less in class. Girls tend to be quiet and well behaved, thinking through their answers carefully before raising their hands. Boys tend to be loud and rowdy; they are more apt to dive right in, calling out an average of eight times more often. In this kind of environment, it's not surprising that teachers focus on the boys or just call on the first person with a hand up, who is usually a boy. What *is* surprising is that teachers tend to accept boys' answers when they call out, but when girls call out, teachers have been found to scold them, telling them to raise their hands first.

Of course, teachers are human. When they were growing up, they learned from their parents and society how boys and girls should act, and some of what they learned is biased by today's more enlightened standards. They may not be aware that they treat girls any differently from the way they treat boys. If they are concerned about sexism and have the best intentions, they may still blow it now and then. This doesn't excuse the behavior, but it can help you understand why they do it.

Textbooks

Thumb through a couple of your schoolbooks. What do you notice? If your books are like those used at many schools, you'll see photos and drawings of boys doing meaningful, challenging, exciting things, while girls help, clean up, or stand around. This is true of preschool-level books and up through books for older kids. In one study of children's picture books, 77 percent of the female characters were doing stereotypically female domestic tasks such as cooking and cleaning. There are probably some pictures in your books that have no girls or women in them, but few or none with no boys or men.

You aren't likely to see women pictured as government officials, scientists, or other leaders (or men pictured as caretakers or homemakers, which is equally unfair). Researchers Lenore Weitzman and Diane Rizzo have found that spelling, math, science, and social studies textbooks show women in a limited number of roles, such as housewife or mother. The words in the books follow the same pattern, frequently excluding girls and women while depicting boys and men as leaders.

In addition, many textbooks present unbalanced views of history or current situations. For example, in 1994, women still represented only 2 percent of the people described in new history textbooks. While it's true that men *have* been more prominent in history than women, female contributions to history have been largely ignored, and the emphasis has been on women's helping men. "When textbooks refer to women being 'given the vote' in 1920 but omit the challenges in that seventy-two-year struggle . . . they are imbalanced," says Susan Crawford in *Beyond Dolls & Guns: 101 Ways to Help Children Avoid Gender Bias.*

Your textbooks may be biased because they were written eons ago or because the authors grew up in a different era. This bias is understandable, but not acceptable. Girls deserve to read books that represent women fairly and provide positive role models.

Name: Shannon Faulkner

First female to: attend a formerly all-male public military school

Preceding events: In 1993, Faulkner applied to the prestigious Citadel, in South Carolina, without disclosing her gender. She was accepted but was later rejected when the school found out she was a woman. After filing a lawsuit that went all the way to the Supreme Court, she became the school's first female cadet in 1995. Although she withdrew after several days of initiation, called "hell week," her actions cleared the way for other women to become cadets.

★★★ GOOD NEWS ★★★

A law called the Gender Equity in Education Act went into effect in 1995. It will provide money for programs to teach teachers about bias, encourage girls in math and science, and help girls of color and low-income girls succeed in school.

Things to Do

OBSERVE A TEACHER

Pay attention in class—not just to what your teacher is saying but also to how he or she runs the classroom. You probably have already noticed any bias. If your teacher is generally fair in responding to boys and girls, that's ideal (in fact, you might want to let him or her know how much you appreciate this). But if you have a teacher who seems to treat you or other girls differently from boys, try to identify a specific thing that seems unfair. For instance, the teacher may say degrading things about women, ignore you when you raise your hand, or leave girls out of class activities.

Once you've zeroed in on a specific thing that's bothering you, consider talking to the teacher about it. Decide whether you think he or she is being rude on purpose or is simply unaware of the behavior. You may want to consult a school counselor or an administrator and ask if he or she thinks the teacher would be sympathetic to criticism. With some teachers, who may not even realize their comments are offensive, your speaking up might open their eyes and help improve the situation. However, other teachers may feel defensive.

New York writer Miranda Van Gelder had a teacher who called all the girls in her class "beautiful, adorable, gorgeous." "I finally confronted him after class one day," Van Gelder wrote in *Ms.* magazine. She explained that his language was sexist and demeaning and "asked if it was really too much to drop all the honey-cookie-pieface-lambchop stuff." Although he was not immediately sympathetic to her view, the important thing is that she conveyed her opinion and potentially paved the way for change in future classes.

If you do feel comfortable approaching the teacher, share your feelings without having too many expectations. Be direct but tactful—think about how you would feel if you were the one being criticized. If your teacher responds positively, great! If he or she doesn't, at least you've done your part by speaking up.

A one-time incident is one thing; continuous offensive comments are another. If talking to the teacher doesn't stop the behavior, or if he or

she is purposely saying offensive things to annoy you, you may want to file a formal complaint with the principal (perhaps after the term is over so there is no question that you get the grade you deserve). The school needs to know if a teacher isn't treating girls fairly. Try to give specific examples and keep track of how often the behavior occurs. Your complaint may not be the first, and the teacher may be reprimanded (in some cases, blatantly sexist teachers have even been fired).

READ YOUR BOOKS

It's time to study—not just the information in your textbooks but how it's presented as well. On page 54 is a checklist you can use to evaluate how your books portray girls and women. Make several copies of this list. Then select one book at a time and check out its text and its illustrations and/or photographs.

EDUCATE OTHERS

Probably the most effective thing you can do to make your school more girl-friendly is to speak your mind. Ask teachers to supplement biased textbooks with nonbiased materials such as magazine articles, write an article about bias in textbooks for the school newspaper, do a class report that focuses on women's contributions to a particular field . . . do whatever you think will help. Sometimes all it takes is a suggestion to start change in motion.

ALERT YOUR SCHOOL

Textbooks must go through an elaborate screening process before they end up on your desk. First the state approves books that school districts can choose from. School districts then form committees that include school staff people and members of the community, and these groups choose the books. If you have a problem with a book, the textbook committee should hear about it. Write a letter to your school board, and send a copy to the state curriculum commission (the address is in the government pages of the telephone book). Who knows? You may influence the committee's decision and do the girls at your school a great service.

WRITE TO A BOOK PUBLISHER

If one of your textbooks needs help in the female representation department, another strategy is to write to the publisher and say you'd like to see a more balanced edition next time. It wouldn't hurt to ask your parents and teachers to do so as well—the publisher might take note if it receives enough mail. (The publisher's address is often listed on the copyright page or can be found in the directory *Books in Print* at your local library.) On the next page is a sample letter.

[date]

Jessie Langer
1415 Georgina
Chicago, IL 48043

Average Publishing
123 Book Square
Minneapolis, MN 64572

Dear Publisher,

I am writing to let you know that I think your book The History of Man *(1996), by John Smith and Steve Jones, is biased against the female half of the population. First of all, the title itself excludes women. Shouldn't it be called* The History of Humanity? *Also, I did an informal survey of the number of male and female figures in the pictures and text, and I found that there a lot more men and boys than women and girls. For instance, on page 101 there is a drawing of five men signing a treaty, and no women or girls are even watching this event. When you show girls and women, they are doing stereotypically female things such as stirring a kettle (page 53) or waving as the men ride horses (page 79). The text contains phrases such as "The men who made America what it is today . . ." which make it sound as though women did not even exist, when in fact they have made major contributions throughout history.*

This type of bias is a serious problem because textbooks help shape girls' impressions of real life. It's important that girls have strong role models to help us believe in ourselves and our abilities. Your book should reflect the way life really was in our country's history.

In the next edition of your book, I would like to see you feature more girls and women in leading roles. You could also show some boys and men in less stereotypical role—for example, preparing meals or helping women. Boys should not have to conform to traditional roles, either. I would also like to see more text that focuses on women's achievements.

Thank you for considering my request. I look forward to seeing the next edition of your book.

Sincerely,
Jessie Langer,
age twelve

PICK UP A GOOD BOOK

You may have to rely on textbooks in certain classes, but they should not be your sole source of learning. To make up for the fact that schoolbooks aren't always the greatest when it comes to how the sexes are portrayed, read some books that feature girls in strong, active roles. Here are examples of fiction that feature preteen and teen girl characters who think and talk about issues such as self-esteem, physical appearance, cultural and social conflicts, family, and history. For more ideas, consult *Great Books for Girls: More than 600 Books to Inspire Today's Girls and Tomorrow's Women* (Ballantine, 1997).

Little Women, by Louisa May Alcott (Little, Brown, 1994).

The True Confessions of Charlotte Doyle, by Avi (Orchard Books, 1990).

Catherine, Called Birdy, and *The Midwife's Apprentice,* by Karen Cushman (HarperCollins, 1995; Clarion, 1995).

Julie of the Wolves and *Julie,* by Jean Craighead George (Harper, 1974 and 1996).

A Girl Called Al, by Constance C. Greene (Puffin, 1991).

Zeely, by Virginia Hamilton (Aladdin, 1993).

The Girl with the White Flag, by Tomiko Higa (Dell, 1992).

The Lilith Summer, by Hadley Irwin (Feminist Press, 1993).

Finding My Voice, by Marie G. Lee (Houghton Mifflin, 1992).

Number the Stars, by Lois Lowry (Dell, 1990).

Letters from a Slave Girl: The Story of Harriet Jacobs, by Mary Lyons (Simon and Schuster, 1996).

Dinah for President, by Claudia Mills (Aladdin, 1992).

Anne of Green Gables, by L. M. Montgomery (Bantam, 1994).

Sarah Bishop, by Scott O'Dell (Scholastic, 1991).

That Crazy April, by Lila Perl (Seabury Press, 1974).

The Maid of the North: Feminist Folk Tales from Around the World, by Ethel J. Phelps (Holt, 1982).

Moon Over Crete, by Jyotsna Sreenivasan (Holy Cow!, 1994).

Shabanu, Daughter of the Winds, by Suzanne Fisher Staples (Knopf, 1989).

Maizon at Blue Hill, by Jacqueline Woodson (Dell, 1994).

HOW FAIR ARE YOUR TEXTBOOKS?

Here is a checklist to help you evaluate your textbooks. Make a copy or write your answers on a separate sheet of paper, and then analyze the results using the section below.

1. How many pictures in the book show only boys or men?____

2. How many pictures show only girls or women?____

3. How many show both boys and girls or men and women?____

4. What are the boys or men in the pictures doing? (List five activities.)

   _____

   _____

   _____

   _____

   _____

5. What are the girls or women in the pictures doing? (List five activities.)

   _____

   _____

   _____

   _____

   _____

6. How many female figures or main characters are included in the book?____

7. How many male figures or main characters are included?____

ANALYSIS

Questions 1–3: Ideally, there should be just as many pictures of females as males in the book. That's only fair. Making girls feel equally represented helps them relate to the subjects being discussed.

Questions 4–5: If the females are always doing passive things, such as helping males or watching them work, the book is biased. Girls should be shown in active roles, because they are just as capable of solving problems and taking charge as boys are. And boys should be shown doing things such as helping a girl with a project or watching something happen—boys don't always have to be in charge.

Questions 6–7: Ideally, a series of textbook word problems should contain an equal number of male and females figures. (But remember that histories of science, math, or politics may not include many female names because in the past very few women were encouraged to pursue careers in these fields.)

Thank You, Ms. Logan

by Josh Haner, fourteen

San Francisco

When I began middle school, I had a teacher named Judy Logan. One of her personal goals was to emphasize women in the curriculum. Her classroom had an amazing assortment of things in it— quilts, posters, and books all on women in our history. Some teachers ignore women's role in our culture, but not Ms. Logan. Instead she stresses female leaders and how they have actually been more important than they seem in our sheltered outlook on history.

For example, when I was in sixth grade, she had us give first-person oral histories of African-American historical figures—one male and one female. We also studied women in science and made a quilt depicting these scientific masters of their time. For one classroom assignment, Ms. Logan had us imagine that we were going back to our birth and were then born as the opposite sex. Later on, when I was in seventh grade, she offered a class on women in history. I decided to sign up, but I silently wondered if I would be the only boy.

The class actually had about the same number of girls and boys and turned out to be something I would remember for a long time. First we listed things that we thought made our gender different from the other, and we then formed two circles. The boys, in the inner circle, read their answers first, while the girls, in the outer circle, listened as a respectful audience. Most of the boys "passed" on reading because we were all too shy to show our true emotions. Then the girls read about what was on their minds. Through this, the boys gained the ability to identify with the opposite sex, knowing what girls go through each day and how their lives are similar to and different from ours. The subject of sexual harassment in schools also came up, and we broke into committees that did investigative studies on it. When the class was over, none of us wanted it to end.

Of all the teachers I've had over the years, Ms. Logan was the one who really made a difference and changed my outlook on life. I also became aware of the struggles that women have gone through to gain their place in society today. Ms. Logan taught me to become sensitive to other people's views. Whether the difference between us is race, religion, or gender, we still deserve the same rights to be heard. So for all of these reasons and more, I would like to say, thank you, Ms. Logan.

"The acceptance of women as authority figures or as role models is an important step in female education. . . . It is this process of identification, respect, and then self-respect that promotes growth."
—*Judy Chicago, artist*

Chapter 7

Math Myths and Science Fiction

Do you like math? How about science?

If you said yes to either or both of these questions, that's great, and this chapter will tell you why. If you said no, you're not alone; many girls share your feelings. But that doesn't mean they—and you—don't have the ability to do well in math and science.

First the bad news: There has been a common notion in America that boys are better at math and science than girls. In a study done about ten years ago, boys scored better than girls on the math college board Scholastic Aptitude Test (SAT), and some experts attributed this difference to superior male ability. However, supporters of equal rights believe that the difference (which studies show is slowly shrinking) between boys' and girls' scores has nothing to do with innate talent and is caused by cultural influences and our educational system. From an early age, boys are conditioned to develop the kinds of problem-solving skills that help with math and science. As a rule, they are encouraged to build things, such as with wood, blocks, or Legos; they are expected to learn how to fix things when they break; and they play video games, which can help build logic and problem-solving skills. They also tend to take more math than girls, so they're better prepared for the math portion of the SAT.

Meanwhile, girls are subtly discouraged from pursuing math and science. They get the message that boys are "naturally" better at fixing things and solving problems, and that girls are better at "people skills" (carrying on a conversation, making others feel comfortable). You may have already noticed ways in which our society speaks to boys' interests and expects girls to listen in. For instance, look at a typical math or science problem in a grade-school book and it will probably say something like: "If Jake has 5 sergeants and Paul has 7 colonels, but Jake later loses a sergeant, how many army men do they have?" Girls may understandably feel put off by this boy-oriented wording and feel less interested in and able to relate to these problems. (See chapter 12, Spread the Word, for more on gender-biased language.)

In addition, some teachers, school counselors, and other adults subtly direct girls away from math and science, instead steering them toward historically female subjects such as home economics and English. As a result, they are likely to become progressively less interested in succeeding in math and science.

However, girls *can* succeed in these areas. Research shows that from a young age, girls understand math and science problems and concepts just as well as boys do—in fact, on average, girls get *better* grades in these subjects. When girls make an effort in math and science, have a chance to develop confidence in their abilities, and are encouraged and helped with the work, they master these subjects with flying colors.

The Payoff

Why should girls explore math and science? Because there is a whole world of fascinating and rewarding job opportunities for girls with strong math and science skills. If you like helping people and want to be a doctor, a science background will help get you into medical school. If you're interested in designing buildings or cities, strong math skills can pave the way for your becoming an architect. If you love animals, a biology background can prepare you to become a veterinarian or a marine biologist. These types of jobs pay much better and have more prestige than most traditionally female jobs such as secretary, retail-clothing salesperson, or salon worker. Math and science skills can also come in handy in other ways and help you function more independently. For instance, they'll be helpful in managing your finances or the family budget (traditionally the responsibility of the "man of the house") or if you choose to run your own business.

So don't give up—stick with your pre-algebra, geometry, physics, biology, and chemistry classes. Chances are good that you *can* do them successfully, enjoy them, and reap their many long-term rewards.

Things to Do

TAKE MATH AND SCIENCE

No matter what you eventually decide to do with your life, it's a good idea to take math and science because it will open up so many job possibilities. Computer programming, for instance, a career that requires math skills, generally pays more than sixty thousand dollars a year, while the average salary for secretarial work is only about twenty-five thousand dollars. Career guidance professionals recommend taking as much math as you can. If you want to go to college, you'll need at least one year of algebra and one of geometry. If you are interested in a science or engineering career, take trigonometry and calculus. One final suggestion: Take these subjects *as early as possible* to give yourself a head start. The sooner you start working with the material, the sooner you'll become comfortable and confident with it.

ASK YOUR TEACHERS FOR HELP

If you are an A or B student in math and science, skip this section. If you aren't, you can increase your chances of succeeding by letting your teachers know you are interested in doing well and by asking for help if you need it. Teachers usually respond positively to students who express a genuine interest in learning material. If they know you care, they'll generally make an extra effort to help you understand the work. If you feel shy about talking to a teacher one-on-one, ask a female classmate to go with you. This will take some of the focus off you and make it more of a group discussion.

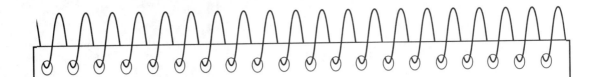

Don't be ashamed to ask for help. Remember, science and math can be challenging for anyone—boys or girls. In their book *All That She Can Be,* authors Carol J. Eagle and Carol Colman note that "it's important for girls to understand that even the brightest students may at times struggle over a particular subject. . . . Asking for help is not a sign of stupidity; rather, it's the smartest thing [you] can do."

ORGANIZE A GIRLS' MATH OR SCIENCE GROUP

Girls often find that it's easier to concentrate on learning math or science when boys aren't around to dominate class discussions—which is what often happens. Some girls do better working one-on-one with other female students and teachers in a relaxed, noncompetitive environment. As a result, schools are starting to form all-girl science or math study groups, and some have even set up all-girl classes.

If you're in a coed math or science class and feel intimidated or ignored, ask some of the other girls if they would be interested in forming a group. Have the group meet during lunch or after school one day a week and go over class material. If you want, find a parent or teacher who is willing to work with you on extracurricular math- and science-related activities. One science group in Newton, Massachusetts, has gone camping, stayed overnight at Boston's Museum of Science, visited a veterinary hospital, gone on nature hikes, collected algae from a pond and studied it under a microscope, and talked to female geology majors at nearby Wellesley College. "I never used to know *why* we were doing science experiments at school," says group member Liz Castellana, fifteen. "What we do in the group shows me that there are reasons for doing the experiments—we think of logical questions and then answer them."

GET INVOLVED IN OPERATION SMART

Operation SMART (which stands for Science, Math, and Relevant Technology) is a national program that helps girls explore math, science, and technical projects. At an Operation SMART center, you can participate with other girls in hands-on projects such as taking apart a computer, doing a chemistry experiment, or building a model city. According to Girls Incorporated, the organization that sponsors the program, these activities help girls "come to see that mistakes aren't failures but opportunities. As they become confident inquirers and explorers, their enthusiasm for science, math, and all learning begins to grow. . . . They learn that they can have power over their lives and change the world around them."

To find out if there is an Operation SMART center near you, contact Girls

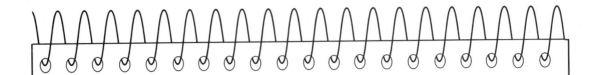

Incorporated, 30 East 33rd St., New York, NY 10016. If there is no center in your area, ask your teacher or a parent if they will start a local chapter.

STUDY FEMALE MATH AND SCIENCE WHIZZES

Do you have a class assignment to study a historical figure? Instead of picking an obvious male, such as George Washington or Albert Einstein, choose a woman scientist or mathematician, such as computer pioneer Grace Hopper or chemist Marie Curie. Not only will you expand your knowledge, but you'll also enlighten your classmates about the accomplishments of this person. While you may not be able to think of many women mathematicians or scientists off the top of your head, there are plenty. To get started, check your local library for the books below.

Celebrating Women in Mathematics and Science, edited by Miriam P. Cooney (National Council of Teachers of Mathematics, 1996).

History of Women in Science for Young People, by Vivian S. Epstein (Epstein, 1994).

Women & Numbers: Lives of Women Mathematicians, Plus Discovery Activities, by Teri Perl (Wide World/Tetra, 1993).

Women Scientists, by Nancy Veglahn (Facts on File, 1992).

Twentieth-Century Women Scientists, by Lisa Yount (Facts on File, 1995).

HOOK UP WITH FRIENDS AND MENTORS

Science by Mail is a program that locates science pen pals for girls and boys in grades four through nine. Participants receive science packets containing directions and materials for doing science experiments; once they've completed an experiment, they report the results to their pen pal. The organization especially encourages girls to join. For information, contact the Museum of Science, Science by Mail, Science Park, Boston, MA 02114; (800) 729-3300.

Want to find out what life is like for real women in high-technology fields, and get to know some of them? If you're a Girl Scout, the International Network of Women in Technology can help. It has a program that matches up professional women in the computer field with members of the Girl Scouts. Contact the network at 4641 Burnet Ave., Sherman Oaks, CA 91403.

EXPLORE COMPUTERS

The computer field offers many opportunities for women, ranging from jobs such as software programmer to on-line service writer. If your family has a computer, start by getting familiar with different word-processing programs, such as Microsoft Word. Try playing around with PhotoShop (a graphics program) or Excel (for creating tables and charts). Ask your parents about subscribing to an on-line service such as Prodigy, CompuServe, or America Online (less than fifteen dollars a month, plus connect time). These services plug you into a huge information network, and

give you access to the even larger Internet. "I put up a question about a science project on one of the electronic bulletin boards, 'Homework Helper,' and got nineteen answers," says Margaret Coit, twelve, of Lexington, Massachusetts. On-line services also enable you to send and receive electronic mail (E-mail) and to talk with other people on-line (be cautious of strange people on-line the same way you would in real life). You may also be able to log on at school or at your local library. "I think all girls should try it," says Coit.

CHECK OUT VIDEO GAMES FOR GIRLS

Girls can now enjoy the brain-strengthening benefits of video games the same way boys do because manufacturers are making games that are interesting and fun for girls. Sega of America has produced various games for girls, as has Electronic Arts, which has one called "Counting On Frank," about a girl who loves math. Other manufacturers include Girl Games (Web site listed below), which has a CD-ROM for girls called *Let's Talk About Me!*, ABC/EA Home Software, Hi Tech Entertainment, Games For Her, and Big Top Productions. Look for girls' video games at video stores and in unexpected places such as girls' clothing stores.

SURF THE NET

Lots of sites on the Internet feature material of special interest to girls. If you have a computer with Internet access, start by checking out these colorful, entertaining, and informative sites:

Club Girl Tech: http://www.girltech.com/

Girl Games: http://www.girlgamesinc.com/

A Girl's World: http://www.agirlsworld.com

Women's History Collaborative Encyclopedia Project:
http://www.teleport.com/~megaines/women.html

Name: <u>Frances Conley</u>

First woman to: become a tenured, full professor of neuro-surgery (brain surgery) in the United States

Preceding events: Conley was a math and science whiz as a girl. She was told she should not pursue a career as a neurosurgeon because "it is too physically demanding, requires too much time, and interferes with having a family." Fortunately she ignored this advice! She currently teaches at Stanford Medical Center, in Palo Alto, California. Her advice to aspiring female scientists? "Hang in there, and don't let anyone dissuade you from your goals. You can make it happen!"

Math Notes

by Robin Beran, age fourteen

Aurora, Colorado

Laurie Sampson

I go to Prairie Middle School in Aurora. My math teacher, Ms. Carpentar, formed a math club, and we compete against other math clubs in the Denver area. Ms. Carpentar is enthusiastic, energetic, and loves math. Miss Johnson, our student teacher, has also helped and encouraged us. At the beginning of the school year, we met once a week to play math games and solve riddles. Later in the year, we competed against other schools. Then came the metro competition. The judges were all people who use math and science every day in various industries. Some of the women had interesting jobs that I had never heard of. One woman worked with computers and made new computer games.

They gave us the toughest test I have ever seen, and I've never worked harder...but Prairie was chosen to go to state competition. What's more, one team got an award for being all girls, and another girl won first place.

I'm not the only girl who likes math!

The Joy of Science

by Doug Kirkpatrick

Walnut Creek, California

I teach eighth-grade physical science at Foothill Middle School, in northern California. Ten years ago, our school started a program called "Computers as Learning Partner" to help kids better understand science. I received funding to get sixteen computers for my classroom.

In the beginning, there were more guys than girls who wanted to use the computers. The teachers involved in the project worked to make sure that we were being gender-neutral and that the materials were not slanted toward the boys. I realized that girls might need more encouragement because of the stereotype that they aren't good at math. I began to really help and encourage the girls, and then there were just as many girls using the computers. I put up classroom displays about successful women in technical fields and named half the computers after famous women scientists.

I have discovered that when it comes to science, girls are every bit as capable as boys. A little encouragement and attention go a long way. Girls I used to have as students have written me letters, thanking me for my support and telling me how they've become scientists or doctors. Obviously it wasn't all my doing, but I'm glad I could help. Here's to their success, and the success of anyone who sets her sights on a career in science.

"It's time that people realize that women in this country can do any job that they want to do."

—Sally Ride, astronaut

★★★ GOOD NEWS ★★★

The winner of the National Outstanding Young Astronomer Award in 1994 was a woman, Stephanie Cinerski. She got interested in science when she was in middle school and decided to enter the science fair competition. Her project: studying sunspots and solar flares over the course of seven years using a telescope, a radio receiver, and other equipment. She studied at Stanford University, in California.

For More Information

Tech Girl's Internet Adventures, by Girl Tech (IDG Books Worldwide, 1997). A guide to the Internet and computer technology from the creators of the award-winning Girl Tech Web site. Age eight and up.

Girls and Young Women Inventing: Twenty True Stories About Inventors, Plus How You Can Be One Yourself, by Frances A. Karnes and Suzanne M. Bean (Free Spirit, 1995). Stories about successful inventors along with tips for creating new products and gadgets yourself.

Great Careers for People Interested in Math and Computers, by Peter and Bob Richardson (Gale, 1993). Includes descriptions of careers, profiles of people in each field, and job outlooks for the future. Grades six to nine.

The Science Book for Girls and Other Intelligent Beings, by Valerie Wyatt (Kids Can Press, 1994). Simple experiments and fun projects that inspire girls to learn about science and careers in science. Ages eight to twelve. Available from the publisher, 29 Birch Ave., Toronto, Ontario, Canada, M4V 1E2.

Fear of Math: How to Get Over It and Get On with Your Life! by Claudia Zaslavsky (Rutgers University Press, 1994). Contains "real-world" math problems and suggests ways to make doing math easier. Age thirteen and up.

Chapter 8
Leave Me Alone!

What would you do if you found out that boys at school were writing sexually oriented graffiti about you in the bathroom? This happened to Katy Lyle of Duluth, Minnesota, when she was fifteen. She told one of the school counselors about it and was told it would be taken care of. But nothing happened. Her brother managed to clean some of the writing off of the stall, but other parts were permanently etched in the metal. Lyle's family got involved, asking sixteen times that something be done about the graffiti. After six months, the school district finally had the bathroom painted. By then, however, Lyle had filed a lawsuit.

Lyle's experience was one form of sexual harassment—unwanted sexual comments or touching at school, during extracurricular activities, or at work. Obviously some incidents of harassment are more serious than others; most don't result in lawsuits. But if the behavior is unwelcome, if you react negatively (as opposed to feeling flattered), and if you have repeatedly asked the person to stop, it's harassment. Generally, it is inappropriate if someone does any of these things:

— Make sexual comments or jokes, use sexual nicknames, or put you down in a sexual way
— Leer at you in a sexual way
— Whistle at you in a sexual way
— Pressure you to engage in unwanted sexual behavior
— Touch or grab you (snapping your bra strap, for example)
— Display pornographic photographs or drawings in public areas
— Make obscene gestures
— Comment about body parts
— Pass sexually explicit notes in class
— Ask about your sexual experience
— Stalk you (follow you against your will)

Sexual harassment should also not be confused with flirting, which usually feels good and is not offensive. "It is the reaction of the harassee, not the intent of the harasser, that is important," says Nan Stein, director of the Sexual Harassment in Schools Project at the Center for Research on Women at Wellesley College.

Most teens say that sexual harassment "happens all the time" at their school. According to a 1993 study by the American Association of University Women, 85 percent of teen girls in public schools have experienced some form of it (in addition, 52 percent of them said *they* have sexually harassed someone). But that doesn't mean it is legal or acceptable. "No matter what you wear or how sexy you look, nobody has the right to sexually harass you," says Harriet Hodgson, author of *Power Plays*, a teen guide to sexual harassment. She chose that title for the book because "sexual harassment isn't about sex—it's about power. . . . The harasser wants to have power over the victim and uses sexuality to achieve this goal."

Spotlight on Harassment

Sexual harassment has been a problem for years, but it wasn't taken very seriously until 1991, when Clarence Thomas was nominated for the United States Supreme Court. During his confirmation process, law professor Anita Hill came forward and said that he had sexually harassed her when she worked for him at the Equal Employment Opportunity Commission. (Ironically, the EEOC is the federal agency that fights discrimination in the workplace.) Hill testified that Thomas would constantly ask her for dates and talk to her about pornographic films. She said she had

been deeply offended by these comments but felt that she could not complain because he was her boss and it could have jeopardized her chances for advancement.

Hill's story sounded believable, and women across the country supported her, but Thomas said it wasn't true. There was a huge public debate—some people believed him, while others believed her. He was confirmed as a justice despite the charge, but Hill had had an effect. In 1992, the Supreme Court itself ruled that if a student can prove she has been sexually harassed, she can sue the school, which was helpful for people like Katy Lyle. In fact, this ruling has already led to one notable case: In 1996, a sixth-grade girl in California named Tianna Ugarte received five hundred thousand dollars to compensate for sexual harassment by a boy in her class. The damages were paid by the school district, the principal, the school, and the harasser's family. Some states have also passed laws against sexual harassment. For instance, Minnesota and California now require that their elementary, junior high, and senior high schools have sexual harassment policies.

Fortunately, many girls have put an end to harassment by simply telling the harasser they don't like it and they want it to stop. Not all harassers realize that what they're doing is offensive—some may think they're "just joking around" or giving you compliments. But the bottom line is not what they think; it's how you feel. "No one has the right to make you feel bad about yourself," says Alicia Treat, thirteen, of Seattle, in *Teen Voices* magazine. "You deserve to be treated with respect like everyone else."

Real-Life Responses

Here are some sample sexual harassment situations and ways girls responded to them, courtesy of the King County Sexual Assault Resource Center:

The scenario: *Janette was carrying her groceries to her car one Saturday afternoon. She noticed a man standing at a pay phone. As she passed him, he interrupted his phone conversation, looked at her, and said, "Nice legs!" Janette ignored his comment, but as she continued walking, he followed her.*

Her response: *She turned and confronted the man, demanding to know what he was doing.*

The scenario: *Sonya was standing at her locker between classes. Her boyfriend, Mark, and a group of his friends approached her. She turned to greet them. Mark cornered her against the lockers, cupping her breast in his hand, and said, "Hey, baby, I'm looking forward to Friday night," as his friends looked on in amusement.*

Her response: *Later that day she spoke to Mark, telling him that what he did made her uncomfortable and that she didn't want him to do it again.*

The scenario: *Lisa had recently begun a new job. Since her first day at work, a number of her male coworkers had made comments about her appearance and inquired about her sexual experience. During a lunch break, one of them, Todd, put his hand on her leg and whispered, "I know what you're looking for" in her ear.*

Her response: *She spoke to another coworker about the incident with Todd. The two of them then met with the supervisor.*

Things to Do

Have you been sexually harassed? If so, how did you react? Maybe you hesitated to say anything because you weren't sure if it was harassment or just lighthearted teasing. Perhaps you shrugged and tried to laugh it off. Maybe you were afraid to say something that might alienate the person.

It's common for girls to hesitate in this kind of situation. But if someone harasses you repeatedly, the person will probably not stop if you simply ignore it. Experts say the best thing to do is ask the harasser to knock it off. You can also describe how the behavior makes you feel or just say that it bothers you. If it would make you feel more comfortable, have a friend, parent, or other adult look on while you talk to the harasser.

If the person doesn't stop after this, the next step is to create a record of the harassment by writing answers to these questions:

☆ What happened?

☆ When did it occur?

☆ Where did it occur?

☆ Were there any witnesses?

☆ What did you say in response to the harassment? (Use exact words if possible.)

☆ How did the harasser respond to you? (Use exact words if possible.)

☆ How did you feel about the harassment?

Make a copy of this written record and take it to the principal, a counselor, or a supervisor if you are at work. Keep your original copy.

If the harassment *still* doesn't stop, the next tactic is to go to a person in higher authority, such as the superintendent of schools or the director of human resources at the company where you work. You can also contact other organizations or people, such as your state's Department of Education or Human Rights or a lawyer. Throughout this process, keep documenting the harasser's behavior and the response of the school or organization. With a little patience, you may well succeed in solving the problem.

MAKE "I" STATEMENTS

An effective tool when confronting someone who is harassing you is to make statements starting with "I" describing your feelings and reactions, says *Power Plays* author Hodgson. If you instead made "you" statements, such as "You're always bothering me," the harasser might feel accused and criticized and would probably respond defensively. But if you simply state your feelings, the harasser will find it hard to verbally attack you. You are not taking responsibility for his behavior; you are just expressing how it affects you.

Here are some examples of "I..." statements, starting with ones for the first time you talk to the person and ending with more aggressive ones. Hodgson recommends that you practice saying the statements out loud so you'll feel comfortable using them.

✿ "I'm having trouble understanding what is going on here."

✿ "I feel uncomfortable when you invade my personal space."

✿ "I don't like being touched by people I hardly know."

✿ "I am insulted by your degrading comments about women."

✿ "I want you to stop sexually harassing me."

✿ "I'll file a complaint if you don't stop sexually harassing me."

HELP OTHERS STOP HARASSMENT

In addition to dealing with harassment directed at you, you can also address harassment of others. There is strength in numbers, and girls who stand together and refuse to tolerate inappropriate behavior increase the pressure for harassment to stop. If you are with or see someone being harassed, and you feel comfortable defending her, say something. Even just mentioning the words "sexual harassment" can have an effect. If you have a friend who is being harassed, offer to be with her if she wants to confront the harasser.

"Dear Harasser..."

Here is a sample letter from a girl to the person harassing her, reprinted from the booklet "Tune In to Your Rights," produced by Programs for Educational Opportunity at the University of Michigan. In the letter, the writer gives specific examples of the harasser's behavior. She then explains how she feels about it and states clearly what she wants to change.

Dear Ken:

I am writing this letter to tell you that I want you to stop bothering me. This is how you are bothering me:

1. Monday, May 14. You and James whistled at me and kept me from going to class. You made rude comments about me.

2. Tuesday, May 15. You passed gross notes to me in Mr. Jacobs's class. You distracted me and I got into trouble because I didn't hear him ask me a question.

3. Wednesday, May 16. I told you to stop picking on me. You ignored what I said and made fun of me in front of your friends. That night I started getting strange phone calls from someone. I think they were from you.

4. Friday, May 18. You lied about me and told your friends that we went out together when we didn't. You said that I was a "hot date." That night you and your friends began driving by my house honking the horn and yelling my name. I think you are trying to ruin my reputation.

Writing this down makes me angry. You are hurting me, and I want you to stop. I want you to: (1) stop whistling at and staring at me; (2) stop calling me rude names; (3) stop acting like I want to see you outside of class; (4) stop telling lies about me; (5) stop calling me on the phone; (6) stop driving by my house; (7) leave me alone.

Michelle

"No one can make you feel inferior without your consent."
—*Eleanor Roosevelt*

★★★ GOOD NEWS ★★★

The United States isn't the only country where sexual harassment has become an important issue in the 1990s. France and Spain have made sexual harassment a criminal offense; the European Community has suggested guidelines for the workplace; and even Japan, where women have historically been seen as second-class citizens, has awarded damages for verbal harassment.

Name: Diane Williams

First woman to: win a lawsuit for sexual harassment by her boss

Preceding events: Williams, who had been a public information aide at the Department of Justice in Washington, D.C., was fired in 1972. In her suit she said she had rejected sexual advances by her boss and that men did not have to face these kinds of situations. In 1976, a U.S. District Court judge agreed and awarded her almost $20,000.

For More Information

Everything You Need to Know about Sexual Harassment, by Elizabeth Bouchard (Rosen Publishing Group, 1994). Focuses on sexual harassment of teens at work.

Sexual Harassment: A Question of Power, by JoAnn Bren Guernsey (Lerner, 1995). A look at the latest developments in the way sexual harassment is defined and how harassees have responded, plus suggestions for handling different scenarios.

Power Plays: How Teens Can Pull the Plug on Sexual Harassment, by Harriet Hodgson (Deaconess Press, 1993). An easy-to-read book that covers all aspects of teen sexual harassment.

"A Blueprint for Action," NOW Legal Defense and Education Fund, 99 Hudson St., New York, NY 10013; (212) 925-6635. A sheet of tips for preventing sexual harassment at school.

"Tune In to Your Rights: A Guide for Teenagers About Turning Off Sexual Harassment," Programs for Educational Opportunity, 1005 School of Education Building, University of Michigan, Ann Arbor, MI 48109-1259. Includes stories from teens. Send your name, address, and a check for three dollars.

"Working Together to Understand and Stop Sexual Harassment," King County Sexual Assault Resource Center, P.O. Box 300, Renton, WA 98057; (206) 226-5062. This booklet features sexual harassment scenarios and dos and don'ts. It's free; just send a self-addressed, stamped envelope and specify the booklet's name.

Infolink, National Victim Center, 309 West Seventh St., Suite 705, Fort Worth, TX 76102; (800) 394-2255. Provides referrals to hotlines and victim service agencies.

Chapter 9
Know the Score

Can you imagine yourself hitting a home run in a pro baseball game or sitting around with a bunch of girlfriends on a Sunday afternoon watching a women's football game on TV? If not, how come? If men and women are ever going to be equal players, the place to start could be on the playing field.

For decades, the big money and media coverage of professional sports have been focused on men's events such as football, basketball, baseball, hockey, and stock car racing. Fewer fans attend women's events or watch them on TV, although tennis, gymnastics, ice skating, and the Olympics are areas where women often hold the spotlight (in the 1992 Winter Olympics, women were the only American athletes to win gold medals). Girls' and women's teams aren't commonly treated as if they are as important as boys' and men's teams. And coaches of women's sports are generally paid less than coaches of men's sports. But these inequities can be changed with a little effort from girls and women.

In fact, a great deal has already changed just in the past twenty years. In 1972, a landmark law called Title IX was passed, requiring that school sports programs give girls and women equal opportunities with boys and men. This means that if your girls' team doesn't get new uniforms but the boys' teams does, or if your team always has to practice in the old gym while the guys practice in the new one, you have grounds for complaint. (It also means boys can be cheerleaders and that cheerleaders are supposed to perform at an equal number of boys' and girls' games.) Before Title IX, there were hardly any athletic scholarships for women, and now there are more than ten thousand. Whereas girls used to be excluded from many sports opportunities, today they have the legal right to join all-boy teams or compete in male-dominated sports. And they are exercising this right: The number of girls playing high school varsity sports has increased 500 percent since 1972. Remember the 1996 Olympics? Female athletes won a record nineteen of America's gold medals, and Title IX was given much of the credit.

Sports Figures

The majority of girls ages eleven to fourteen (84 percent) are involved in sports. If you're not already an athlete, ask a girl who is how she likes it—she'll probably be pretty enthusiastic. Being an athlete can give you a sense of your own power, both physical and mental. Studies show that female athletes are more self-reliant and get better grades and higher test scores than girls who don't participate in sports. Sports can help you develop skills that will be useful later in your life, such as working as part of a team and competing to do your best. According to one survey, 95 percent of top-level executives at *Fortune* 500 companies said they had participated in a high school sport. Being an athlete also builds your physical strength, helps you stay healthy and relieve stress, gives you opportunities to make new friends, and, if you're talented, can help you get into college. Last but not least, sports are fun, according to 58 percent of the girls questioned in one survey.

To sum up, participating in sports can go a long way toward helping you stand up for yourself. The skills you develop can teach you that you count and help you develop self-confidence so you won't let yourself be pushed around. If you haven't already, join the team!

"I am a pioneer, and sports is my frontier. . . . I'm muscular, but that strength and endurance enhances, not diminishes, my femininity. I can wear six-inch nails and one-legged bodysuits and set world records. And leave a lot of men in the dust."
—*Florence Griffith-Joyner, track star*

Girls Can't Throw

by Mariah Burton Nelson

Arlington, Virginia

Betsy Webster/Salty-Web Studios

I have heard a lot of dumb questions and comments about girls in sports. Since I'm a female athlete, I've come up with a few of my own answers—some snappy, some just smart. Try using them the next time you hear a stupid thing like . . .

"Baseball is for boys."
Is Victoria Brucker a boy? No, but Victoria, twelve, pitched in the Little League World Series. Is Julie Croteau a boy? No, but she played college baseball. Even way back in 1931, a woman named Jackie Mitchell pitched for the Chattanooga Lookouts, a men's team. (In a game against the Yankees, she struck out both Babe Ruth and Lou Gehrig.) And in the 1940s and 1950s, there was a women's professional league called the All-American Girls' Baseball League. In the 1990s, a team of women called the Colorado Silver Bullets began touring the country, playing against men.

"Football is for boys."
Then how come more than five hundred girls in five different states play high school football each year?

"Girls who play sports wish they were boys."
No, but we wish we had all the chances guys have to play sports—and all the support they get from other people. We wish that we could see women athletes on television more often. We wish there were more women coaches.

"You throw like a girl."
Gee, thanks for the compliment. Actually, there is no *female* style of throwing. Girls can throw balls just as well as boys. When girls or boys don't throw well, it's only because no one ever taught them how to do it.

"Boys are better athletes than girls."
Tell that to race car driver Lyn St. James, jockey Julie Krone, or dogsled racer Susan Butcher. Each has beaten men in dozens of races. In riflery, horseback riding, and many more sports, women and men compete equally. Female runners, swimmers, and tennis players have defeated men. It happens every day, in all sorts of sports: Sisters beat brothers; girlfriends beat boyfriends. Usually what matters is how much a person practices, not whether the person is a guy or a girl.

"Well, males are stronger than females."
OK, there are differences. Glad you noticed. But up until junior high or so, some girls are just as strong as—or even stronger than—boys. Since most guys develop big muscles during puberty, they tend to be good at sports such as weight lifting and football. Some grow taller than girls, which helps them in volleyball and basketball. Girls, who usually are shorter and lighter and have more body fat than boys, tend to be better at horse racing, gymnastics, and cold-water swimming. But do girls try to keep boys off horses or out of the water? Of course not. It doesn't matter who's the best at a sport, just that everyone gets a chance to play and get better.

"Boys don't like you if you beat them at sports."
Nobody likes to lose. Besides, not all guys feel that way, and why should we care about the ones who are so immature that they can't stand to be beaten?

....

Mariah Burton Nelson is the author of The Stronger Women Get, the More Men Love Football!

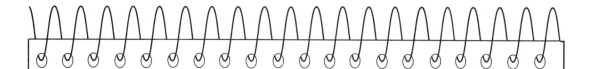

Things to Do

SUIT UP

There are probably several sports you could participate in at school and in your community. If you think you would enjoy competing as a member of a team, you might like basketball, soccer, volleyball, field hockey, or softball. If you like the idea of being on a team but also want to compete as an individual, consider track and field, cross-country, tennis, swimming, diving, sailing, martial arts, or golf. If you think you would enjoy sports most when you're not winning or losing but just playing, consider hiking, skating, or bicycling. And if you don't think you actually want to *play* a sport but do want to be involved, consider volunteering to keep score for your favorite girls' team, being a bat girl, or writing about local athletic events for your school newspaper.

If you fall into the competitive category and want to not only play a sport but also excel at it, set goals, visualize yourself reaching them, and work hard. Start with a goal you know you can reach, such as scoring a certain amount of points per game or running a specific number of miles, and then increase it when you reach it. For inspiration, think of other girls who have achieved success in sports, such as swimmer Amanda Beard, fifteen, of California, who won three medals at the 1996 Summer Olympics; Kendra Wecker, twelve, of Kansas, who was the first female finalist in the National Football League Punt, Pass, and Kick competition (1995); and another Kansan, Laurie Koehn, who won a 1996 national basketball competition, beating both male and female state champions at shooting baskets.

START A GIRLS' TEAM

Does your school lack a girls' team for the sport you like most? You may be able to start a team, provided that enough other girls want to play. First talk to the director of the athletic department or a P.E. teacher to discuss the idea. Would your team play against the boys' team, or is there a girls' league in the area? Would the school provide a coach, uniforms, and equipment if enough girls sign up? (Remember that Title IX requires schools to give girls equal opportunities in sports.) Then start recruiting players. Write a notice about the prospective team for the school newspaper and post a flyer and sign-up sheet on a bulletin board in the locker room. Wait a couple of weeks so word can get out, and when you've got enough players, schedule an introductory meeting to plan your season.

RALLY SUPPORT FOR YOUR TEAM

Are you on a girls' team that has fewer fans at games than the equivalent boys' team? You may be able to change this imbalance. Approach the head of the athletic department or a P.E. teacher. Ask him or her to work with you to promote your team's games. Talk to the editor of the school or community newspaper to find out if the paper could do a feature on the team and list the game schedule. Get the team to come up with a fun T-shirt design, and have everyone wear the shirts on game days. Ask your friends to tell everyone about your games. If you hold a fund-raiser for the team, go all out to publicize it. Get creative: Are there other ways you might be able to attract a larger audience? Once people are aware that the girls' team is playing and the games are fun to watch, attendance is likely to increase.

JOIN A BOYS' TEAM

An all-girl team is one way to go; a coed team is another. If this idea sounds interesting to you, give it a shot, but be prepared for some resistance from the boys. "Some boys think girls are trying to outdo them in their sport, and that is a threat," says Meghan Gagliardi, thirteen, who joined a coed hockey team in Thunder Bay, Ontario. "They're afraid you might be better than they are." As a result, they may behave immaturely—make fun of you, try to trip you, not pass the puck to you, or generally try to make your experience miserable so you'll quit the team. Gagliardi says that the first year she played, she wasn't very good. "The boys teased me and had this attitude like, 'You're a girl—you shouldn't even be here!' " she says. "They would trip me, and I would think, *Why am I doing this?*"

In this situation, the best tactic is to concentrate on playing the sport. Once you've stuck with it for a while, others will begin to appreciate your determination and ability. This was certainly the case for Gagliardi. She continued playing hockey for two years and improved her skills considerably. The same boys who snubbed her are now her friends. "My team accepts me as just another team member now," she says.

A Goal for the Girls

One afternoon Rachel Rief watched in disbelief as her second-grade teacher handed out sign-up sheets for a new soccer team only to the boys in the class. "It really ticked me off," says Rachel, twelve years later. "So I snagged one of the sheets and took it home." That night she asked her father to make copies of the form, and the next day she recruited her classmates for a new girls' team, coached by her dad. "We lost every game that season," Rachel says, "but we had so much fun."

Rachel wasn't the only girl in Yakima, Washington, who was passionate about soccer. Her best friend, Margaret Kowalsky, had been playing since kindergarten. For the next several years, the two girls played on teams and attended soccer camps. But as they got older, Rachel and Margaret were increasingly in the minority. Most campers were boys, and the coaches, without exception, were men. For most girls, soccer took a backseat to "boys, makeup, and cheerleading," remembers Rachel. "Margaret and I thought how different it would be if there were women role models."

So three years ago, the girls launched FUNdamentals Summer Soccer Camp Just-For-Girls. At twenty-two dollars per player, the camp—two weeklong morning programs every August—doesn't provide much more than schoolbook money for its coaches. "We make less than we'd make baby-sitting," admits Margaret. "But two sessions is as big as it's going to get. It's more fun this way."

In addition to lessons in soccer skills and teamwork, Rachel says, "we're showing that women are smart, go to college, are best friends, and enjoy each other." The first summer, forty girls signed up; by last year attendance had almost tripled.

Now college sophomores on opposite coasts—Rachel at Gonzaga University, in Spokane, Washington, and Margaret at Wellesley College, in Wellesley, Massachusetts—the girls plan to offer FUNdamentals again this summer. But at some point, both concede, their lives may move in different directions and the camp will pass on to the next generation. No problem: They've already recruited several younger girls as junior coaches.

—by Maggie Jones; first appeared as "Smart Cookies" in *Working Woman*, April 1995

★★★ **GOOD NEWS** ★★★

A study sponsored by the Women's Sports Foundation found that high school girls who play sports are 92 percent less likely than nonathlete girls to be involved with drugs and 80 percent less likely to have an unwanted pregnancy.

Name: <u>Billie Jean King</u>

First woman to: beat a man in a professional tennis match

Preceding events: In 1973, fifty-five-year-old former tennis champion Bobby Riggs challenged King to a match. With more than thirty thousand people watching live and sixty million watching the contest on TV, she beat him (6–4, 6–3, 6–3).

For More Information

In These Girls, Hope Is a Muscle, by Madeleine Blais (Grove/Atlantic, 1995). The true story of a girls' high school basketball team trying to win the state championship. For older girls.

Champions: Stories of Ten Remarkable Athletes, by Bill Littlefield (Little, Brown, 1993). Includes profiles of marathon winner Joan Benoit-Samuelson, dogsled racer Susan Butcher, and jockey Julie Krone.

A Whole New Ball Game: The Story of the All-American Girls' Professional Baseball League, by Sue Macy (Holt, 1993). Chronicles the period from 1943 to 1954, when women played professional baseball.

Winning Ways: A Photohistory of American Women in Sports, by Sue Macy (Holt, 1996). A look at 150 years of women in sports: what they wore, how they behaved, and how they were regarded, including photographs.

A Sporting Chance, by Andy Steiner (Lerner Publications, 1995). Addresses issues that girl athletes face and looks at the costs, benefits, and opportunities of a "level playing field."

Outstanding Women Athletes, by Janet Woolum (Onyx Press, 1992). Features biographies of sixty Olympic or world-champion female athletes.

Sports Illustrated for Kids, (800) 992-0196.

"Kids Packet," Women's Sports Foundation, Eisenhower Park, East Meadow, NY 11554; (800) 227-3988. A free guide for girl athletes that includes facts about women athletes, tips on keeping in shape, and quizzes.

National Association for Girls & Women in Sport, 1900 Association Dr., Reston, VA 22091; (703) 476-3400 or (800) 213-7193. This organization works to achieve equity in athletics at all levels. Write or call for a list of publications.

Our Society

Chapter 10
Media Darling

Suppose you're an alien who's just landed on Earth, somewhere in the United States. Wanting to find out what the strange-looking humans are like, you turn on the TV. What conclusions do you draw?

You probably get the impression that most females are young, white, and slender, with smooth skin and shiny hair, and that they don't do or say much. You are likely to conclude that mothers easily work full-time and cook gourmet meals for their families every night, and that their biggest joy in life is having a spotless home.

Of course these observations wouldn't reflect real life. But many people—without even realizing it—take media portrayals as a representation of how life should be. And this is troubling because the media—not just TV, but movies, newspapers, and magazines—is generally biased against girls and women. For example, newspapers feature mostly stories about men, written by men—only 15 percent of front-page newspaper references are about women. Only about 30 percent of TV news reporters are women, and only 24 percent of the people interviewed on the nightly news are women or girls.

Of course, government and business are still dominated by men, and this imbalance explains some of the bias. But women and their events and concerns seldom get the coverage or respect they deserve. In fact, in news pieces about women or girls, men are often the "experts" quoted! Many stories aimed at female readers are trivial or inane, such as magazine articles devoted to putting on makeup or choosing the right shampoo. As insulting as such articles are, many women's magazines print them because advertisers demand editorial material that helps sell their products.

Then there are television shows. Male characters outnumber female characters three to one on prime-time TV. In children's programs, only a fourth of the characters are female. Girls Incorporated sums up what girls see on TV: "Girls are portrayed as weak followers who need boys to make their decisions; popular only if they are beautiful, thin, weak, compliant, and not too bright; victims of male violence and dominance; preoccupied with their looks, domestic chores, and bonding with boys." Movies also need more girls and women in active roles. For example, have you seen the Walt Disney movie *Toy Story?* Its large cast of characters features only two female toys, and they are insignificant to the plot. The writers easily could have included more strong female role models.

There's no law that says the media has to be fair, but there is a good reason for it to be: Women are not a minority population, as is implied by the phrase "women and minorities"; we are *more than half of the population.* We need more news and entertainment about us, or reported or produced by us, featuring us, in a way that respects who we are. "We don't need advice on how to firm our thighs," notes Media Watch, a media-monitoring group in Santa Cruz, California. "We need substantive articles and diverse role models to help create a world where women can begin to experience their inalienable rights to freedom and happiness!"

Write a Letter

by Jane Garland Katz

New York

L. Ella Gant

I wrote my first letter to the editor of a newspaper when I was fourteen. It was 1968, and my local newspaper had censured the singer Eartha Kitt for speaking against the Vietnam War during a White House luncheon. That made me mad.

My letter was printed . . . and my fate as a letter writer was sealed. I felt that by participating I had become a true citizen in the world's greatest democracy.

Girls' voices need to be heard. But other than wearing a campaign button or a T-shirt, how can you be sure you *will* be heard? Writing a letter may be your most effective tool. Public policy is affected by opinion—your opinion. You don't need to know big words to make a difference. You just need an opinion.

The next time you read something that disturbs or disheartens you, or even something you feel good about and want to encourage, write a letter. Regardless of whether it is published, by having taken the time to write, you will have sent a clear and powerful message to those who mold social and political attitudes and who are responsible for accurately informing the public. That's the first step toward change, and change will do girls good.

Jane Garland Katz is a writer who has authored many articles for magazines. She lives in New York City.

Magazine Mirages

by Barbara Stretchberry

Greeley, Colorado

Amy Baird

The media has such a powerful influence on our lives because we like the fantasy images it gives us. But sometimes this power gets out of control, and we forget who we really are, and instead obsess about who we *should* be.

I subscribed to my first magazine, *Young Miss* (before *YM*), when I was eleven or twelve. When I was older, I graduated to *Seventeen* and all the other "fashion" magazines I could get my hands on. What I loved most were all the articles on guys—I had never had a boyfriend, so those articles were all so intriguing to me. Through the magazines, I got to pretend that I was someone else—like I had a boyfriend. I also liked the beauty tips; I wanted to be the most gorgeous student in the world. But no matter how much I curled my hair or how much money I spent on makeup, I still had my same body, and I still hated it. And I still didn't have a boyfriend—something I thought every girl should have—at least that's what the magazines were telling me.

I stopped reading those crazy rags when I started college. Now I just take them apart—literally. I take my scissors and cut up the pages and rearrange the words. I destroy the illusion of the models' perfect, airbrushed beauty. This lets me realize the media's influence and not let it control me. Looking at the magazines with this new perspective gives me a sense of control. I don't have to let anyone else dictate the meaning of the words *glamour, vogue,* and *cosmopolitan* to me. I can define them myself.

Barbara Stretchberry wrote her college thesis on girls and the media.

Things to Do

By reading the introduction to this chapter, you've already done something constructive, and that's simply to be aware that the media world and the real world don't always match. "It's important for girls to explore the impact the culture has on their growth and development," says Mary Pipher, author of the bestselling book *Reviving Ophelia: Saving the Selves of Adolescent Girls.* "Once girls understand the effects of the culture on their lives, they can fight back." In other words, knowledge is power. The more you know, the less you'll be taken in by the media.

One way to increase your awareness is to informally rate the news media on its inclusion of women and girls. How do you tell if magazine, newspaper, or TV coverage is biased? According to Fairness and Accuracy in Reporting (FAIR), a national media-monitoring organization, some telltale things to look for include:

✿ News is reported from a male point of view, or with a focus on how men are affected.

✿ Very few women, compared to men, are interviewed or quoted.

✿ Different standards are used for women and men. For example, sports announcers sometimes comment on women's looks but rarely on men's.

✿ The important stories are reported by men.

✿ Gender stereotypes are used. For example, stories about welfare frequently show women, although plenty of men are on welfare.

When you run across some news that you think is reported in a biased way—or if you're pleasantly surprised by a story's fairness—what can you do about it? Write a letter, of course. Get the media organization's address, and send in your two cents' worth. Here are a few letter-writing suggestions:

✿ Start by citing the article or story, the author or reporter, and the date the story appeared.

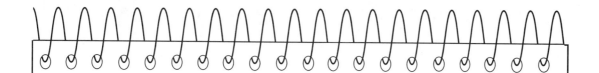

☼ Include your name, address, and telephone number so the editor can contact you to verify who you are.

☼ Mention a related personal experience if you've had one. For example, if you see an ad on TV that shows girls "playing dumb" but you and your friends don't act that way, point that out.

☼ Send your letter to the attention of "Reader Service Editor" or "Letters to the Editor" if it's a newspaper or magazine, or "Manager" if it's a TV or radio station. The major TV network addresses are listed on the next page. If your family has access to an on-line computer service, you can also send E-mail to certain magazines and newspapers.

TUNE IN TO TV

When it comes to female stereotypes, television is one of the worst offenders, says fifteen-year-old Lindsay Glesener, an editor at *New Moon: The Magazine for Girls and Their Dreams,* in Duluth, Minnesota. To begin with, there aren't many strong role models for girls on TV. Very few prime-time programs have a plot about a female character's academic pursuits or career plans. Women are commonly shown in traditional or stereotyped roles (for example, as secretaries, housewives, or sex objects). For example, Glesener sites the show *Baywatch,* in which the characters "wear such minimal clothing." She adds, "These are the sort of things our magazine is trying to stop. We've gotten letters from girls all over the world who are concerned and want to do something about the media."

Here's a media analysis project. Make several copies of this questionnaire, and use them to keep track of what roles men, women, girls, and boys play in a few different TV shows.

Name of show _____
Lead female character's name _____
Her occupation/role _____
Her personality traits _____
Her problems and dilemmas _____

Lead male character's name _____
His occupation/role _____
His personality traits _____
His problems and dilemmas _____

Based on this information, rate each of the shows on a scale of 1 to 10 for gender bias or stereotyping (1 is no bias; 10 is an extreme amount of bias).

Your best-rated show: _____ Rating: _____
Your worst-rated show: _____ Rating: _____

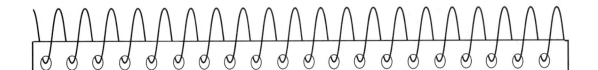

Pass along the results of your analysis to the networks that air these shows. Address your letter to each network's Office of Broadcast Standards and Practices. Explain why you think your worst-rated show needs to improve the way it portrays women. Then say why your top-rated show won your approval. Here are the addresses:

ABC

East Coast:
77 W. 66th St.
New York, NY 10023-6298
(212) 456-7777

West Coast:
2040 Avenue of the Stars
Century City, CA 90067
(213) 557-7777

CBS

East Coast:
51 W. 52nd St.
New York, NY 10019
(212) 975-4321

West Coast:
7800 Beverly Blvd.
Los Angeles, CA 90036
(213) 852-2345

NBC

East Coast:
GE Building, 30 Rockefeller Plaza
New York, NY 10112
(212) 664-4444

West Coast:
3000 Alameda Ave.
Burbank, CA 91523
(818) 840-4444

Fox
c/o Twentieth Century Fox Film Corp.
10201 W. Pico Blvd.
Los Angeles, CA 90035
(310) 369-1000

START A PHONE TREE

Girls Incorporated has a program called Girls Re-Cast TV, which helps girls see how the media affect them. One of the group's recommended projects is to start a phone tree, a network of girls who respond to media bias. To start a tree, write down the names of two or more friends you will call when you see something you don't like about how women or girls are portrayed on TV. Then ask each of these girls to write down two or more names of people they will call, and have those people ask for two more names apiece, and so on (sort of like the way a chain letter works). When any of you see something of interest on TV—either good or bad—call your "branches" and have them call theirs so you can all watch and evaluate it. Then have everyone write or call the responsible network, and you'll have a much bigger impact!

Girls Incorporated recommends simplifying this process by assembling a media-monitoring kit to keep near the TV: a box (preferably with a lid) that includes stationery or writing paper, envelopes, pens, stamps, addresses, and telephone numbers (send for a handy brochure from the Screen Actors Guild, listed on page 91), and your phone tree contact list. "If the show is really degrading or damaging, every girl on the phone tree should go to her media-monitoring kit and write a letter," recommends Girls Incorporated. The more letters the network gets, the less likely it will be to rebroadcast the show or air a similar one.

LISTEN TO LYRICS

You've probably noticed that some rock and rap music has lyrics that are hostile toward women. While free-speech advocates say that bands should be able to sing anything they want, and although you may focus on the *sound* of the music anyway, some people believe that these lyrics make contempt for and violence against women seem commonplace and acceptable. "We don't have to look far in a music store to find music that degrades women and promotes bigotry," says David Walsh, author of *Selling Out America's Children*. "Many lyrics by heavy metal bands are blatantly sexist, racist, and violent." Music videos compound the problem by adding offensive visuals and gestures.

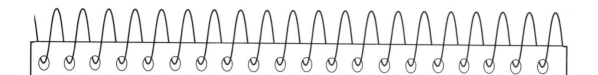

If the words to a particular song offend you, write to the company that produced the CD (the address should be printed on the inside flap of the liner). Circle or write down the lyrics. Tell the company why you find them offensive, and note that you don't plan to buy any more of the group's CDs. If you are offended by a music video, contact the station on which you saw it played:

The Box
1221 Collins Ave.
Miami Beach, FL 33139
(305) 674-5000

MTV
1515 Broadway, 24th floor
New York, NY 10036
(212) 258-8000

VH1
1515 Broadway
New York, NY 10036
(212) 258-7800

One-Girl Revolution

Animated and liberated, Lisa Simpson wages a one-girl revolution against cartoonland patriarchy every week on Fox TV's The Simpsons, created by Matt Groening. Whether she's marching for gay rights, subverting Thanksgiving with a tribute to forgotten foremothers, or demanding equal pay for equal work during household chores, Lisa's personal is intensely political. She told Ms. that role models like Simone de Beauvoir and George Eliot fueled her feminism, as did "the off chance that my father, Homer, and my brother, Bart—much as I love them—represent a fair cross section of American men." In her crusade against sexism, Lisa recently took on the makers of the talking Malibu Stacy doll—who exclaims, "I wish they taught shopping in school." She marketed her own Lisa Lionheart doll, who tells girls, "Trust in yourself and you can achieve anything!" Despite her desire to one day be chief justice or president of the U.S., Lisa says, "I imagine that in twenty years—as during the past five seasons—I shall find myself still in the second grade at Springfield Elementary." But to her live-action sisters, she urges: "Go forth to third grade! And beyond! I'm counting on you."

—**from Ms. magazine**

<u>Name</u>: Dale Messick

First female to: have a syndicated cartoon strip

Preceding events: Dalia Messick shortened her name to Dale so newspaper editors wouldn't know she was a woman and then wrote a comic strip called <u>Brenda Starr.</u> It was the first comic strip with a female main character, and it began running in the <u>Chicago Tribune</u> in 1940. Today there are many more successful female cartoonists, including Cathy Guisewite, Nicole Hollander, and Lynda Barry.

For More Information

Don't Be a TV: Television Victim, written by Ann Simonton, directed by Jenai Lane. Kids narrate this video, which exposes stereotypes in the media and advertising and outlines actions you can take. Kindergarten to eighth grade. Available from Media Watch (see page 114).

Screen Actors Guild, Affirmative Action Department, 5757 Wilshire Blvd., Los Angeles, CA 90036-3600; (213) 549-6644. Publishes a free brochure listing TV networks and the people to contact at each of them, plus addresses for motion picture studios and major advertisers.

Recommended Publications

Blue Jean Magazine: For Teen Girls Who Dare, P.O. Box 90856, Rochester, NY 14609; (716) 654-5070. Teen girls and women are the authors of this magazine's upbeat articles related to activism, careers, and women's history.

Empowered Young Females, P.O. Box 1296, Colorado Springs, CO 80901; (888) 833-6624 (777-1892 in Phoenix); http://www.eyf.com. A colorful magazine with girl staffers that covers topics from self-awareness to sports and careers.

Girls' Life, 4517 Harford Rd., Baltimore, MD 21214; (410) 254-9200. Deals with all aspects of girlhood, including self-esteem, sports, and entertainment.

The New Girl Times, 215 W. 84th St., New York, NY 10024; (800) 560-7525. This newspaper staffed by girl reporters includes short articles on a wide variety of topics, as well as columns, book reviews, and cartoons.

New Moon: The Magazine for Girls and Their Dreams, P.O. Box 3587, Duluth, MN 55803-3587; (218) 728-5507; http://www.cp.duluth.mn.us/~newmoon/. This award-winning, advertising-free magazine run by girls features stories, comments, and art by contributors from all over the world.

Teen Voices: The Magazine by, for and about Teenage and Young Adult Women, Women Express, P.O. Box 6009, JFK Post Office, Boston, MA 02114; http://www.1USA1.com/womenexp/. Ideally suited for older girls (age fifteen and up), this publication tackles such issues as teen motherhood, racism, addictions, and personal loss.

Chapter 11
The "Old Boys' Club"

Can you name a past woman president of the United States?

Of course not! There haven't been any. However, if the predictions of Patricia Aburdene and John Naisbitt, authors of *Megatrends for Women,* are right, we could elect a female president by the year 2008.

This would be a substantial accomplishment considering the brief history of women in politics. Women won the right to vote only in 1920, after decades of struggle. Since then, more and more women have been elected to public office. One milestone occurred in 1984, when presidential candidate Walter Mondale chose a woman, Geraldine Ferraro, as his running mate. Women now make up 11 percent of the House of Representatives and 9 percent of the Senate, as well as about 21 percent of the law-makers in state legislatures.

But that's not very much, you're probably thinking. You're right! And if you turn on CNN and watch a congressional session, you'll see that it's still primarily men who debate,

LOOK GUYS... WHY DON'T WE JUST SAY THAT ALL MEN ARE CREATED EQUAL... AND LET THE LITTLE LADIES LOOK OUT FOR THEMSELVES?

write, and pass the laws—including ones that mainly affect women, such as child care legislation. Because of this gender imbalance, the Senate is still aptly called the "Old Boys' Club."

One sign of hope is that there are ten million more American women registered to vote than men. This means that women have the power to greatly influence many elections. But so far, female voters haven't necessarily voted for female candidates, even if their views have been similar. Some women say that they prefer to vote the same way their husbands do. Others don't realize that women in office are generally more likely to pass laws that help women and girls.

It's critical that women and girls have more pro-female leaders. Of course, male politicians can advocate for women's concerns, but according to the Center for the American Woman in Politics, female officeholders are more likely to give priority to policies and laws focused on women's rights. What's more, women's unique perspectives and brains are a crucial national asset. "It just doesn't make sense not to utilize the talents, creativity, and energies of one half the population in solving the problems facing America today," explains George Dean, founder of 50/50 by 2000, a group that is trying to bring more women into politics. "To deny leadership positions to women is not only shortsighted; it can also severely limit the potential of our people, both male and female." The more girls understand what vital roles they'll be able to play in the political process—whether by simply voting or by running for office—the better off our country's female population will be. It is important to note that although the United States is lagging when it comes to women in office, some other countries have better records. A few examples: Lawyer Mary Robinson, president of Ireland, has been in office since 1990, and Gro Harlem Brundtland, the first female prime minister of Norway, has been at her post since 1981.

Before women won the right to vote in 1920, many men were opposed to sharing this privilege with the opposite sex.

How I Became Governor

by Ann Richards

former Texas governor

Texas Capitol Press Office

When I was a girl taking "vocational preference" tests, I never saw the career choice of "politician" on any of them. That's because the girls were given different tests from the boys, so the choices were predictably limited: If our answers indicated an interest in people or their problems, the choice was something like social worker or nurse, not politician. But what better way is there to serve people than to go into public service?

I got interested in politics in high school, when I attended Girls State, a camplike workshop on local government, and Girls Nation, the Washington counterpart. After high school, I worked in a volunteer capacity in numerous local election campaigns. I had never thought nor hoped to run for office myself. Women were not allowed roles of responsibility beyond licking stamps or making copies, no matter how much experience or education we had. It was my husband who insisted that we alter our lifestyle and invest time and money in my pursuit of public office. I was elected county commissioner in Travis County in 1976 and eventually became governor, in 1990.

Many people in government service whom I visited when I was county commissioner said that they had never been called on by a government official before. They couldn't believe I was truly interested in their agency or department. Some women fear that they lack experience, but our interest and willingness to give of ourselves far surpasses that of the male officeholders who have gone before us.

An increasing number of women are finding that politics offers us an opportunity to act on what we think. We've decided to *do* rather than to *observe*. The contributions of women in government have figured significantly in making the United States a better place. For example, I and other women officeholders have worked to make government inclusive rather than exclusive. We have worked to bring in those citizens who have been previously left out of the power structure: men and women from all walks of life and viewpoints.

Now it is up to young women and girls to seize new leadership opportunities. Then when the question is raised (as it was in my campaign) if a woman can be governor (or city council member, or mayor, or president), the answer will be "Why not?"

Name: Wilma Mankiller

First woman to: be elected chief of the Cherokee Nation of Oklahoma

FIRST FEMALE

Preceding events: In 1957, the Bureau of Indian Affairs moved Mankiller's family from a rural part of Oklahoma to San Francisco. She began doing volunteer work in the local Cherokee community and went on to direct a Native American Youth Center and cofound an alternative school. This experience helped prepare her to lead the Cherokee Nation from 1985 to 1995. She is credited with improving people's lives through creating better health care services and prospects for education, training, and employment.

Things to Do

You may be too young to vote, but you can still make your voice heard on issues that matter to you. Many activist organizations have teen members who help support laws, organize rallies, or work to inform the public about various issues. Joining them is an effective way to get involved, because group efforts often get more attention than individual ones. In fact, much of the recent progress in women's rights is thanks to groups such as the National Organization for Women (NOW), whose members express their opinions by leafletting, holding marches, picketing, protesting, and organizing letter-writing campaigns.

Here are several women's rights organizations that have teen members. Contact them for more information about what they do, and ask whether they have a chapter near you.

✿ *National Organization for Women (NOW)*, 1000 16th St. NW, Suite 700, Washington, DC 20036; (202) 331-0066. The best-known organization advocating for women's rights in the United States.

✿ *Third Wave Direct Action Corp.*, 116 East 16th St., 7th Floor, New York, NY 10003; (212) 388-1898. This group of young women was founded to get young people more involved socially and politically in their communities.

✿ *Young Women's Project*, 933 F St. NW, 3rd Floor, Washington, DC 20004; (202) 393-0461. A "multicultural advocacy and action organization" that helps young women through education and community organizing.

You can also make an impact and gain experience for a future career in politics by working with a group that focuses on some other issue, such as protecting the environment. Here are a few groups that have teen members:

✿ *National Coalition for the Homeless,* 1612 K St. NW, Suite 1004, Washington, DC 20006; (202) 775-1322. Advocates for ending homelessness.

✿ *National Wildlife Federation,* 8925 Leesburg Pike, Vienna, VA 22184; (703) 790-4000. This group focuses on conservation and education about saving endangered species. Call to find out if there is a local chapter near you.

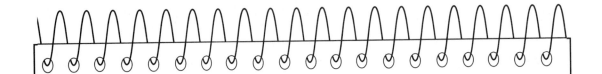

✿ *Natural Resources Defense Council,* 40 West 20th St., New York, NY 10011; (212) 727-2700. One of the most well known environmental advocacy organizations.

For a comprehensive list of organizations, consult *The Kid's Guide to Social Action,* by Barbara Lewis (Free Spirit, 1991).

HELP A CANDIDATE

Volunteering to help a woman who is running for office is a great way to find out if the world of politics might be for you. How do you find a candidate you'd like to support? First determine whether it's an election year, which occurs every two years. If it is, ask your parents and teachers for suggestions, read the newspaper, watch the news, or call city hall and ask for the names and phone numbers of local female candidates. Call one or more of them and ask the campaign workers what the candidate supports.

If she is concerned about women's rights and other issues that you consider important, ask if she needs any volunteers.

You might be asked to call voters, go door-to-door (usually with someone else) to hand out brochures and talk about the candidate, or simply answer the phone, stuff envelopes, and run errands. This may not seem like much, but volunteers play an important role in campaigns. As U.S. Representative Lynn Woolsey attests, "The hard work and dedication of truly committed individuals is one of the main reasons I am in Congress today."

WRITE TO YOUR REPRESENTATIVES

Government leaders may pass the laws, but they have to answer to their constituents—the people in their districts, including young people. If they don't, they won't get reelected. If you have an opinion to voice, you can write or call your local and state representatives, or anyone else who is involved with a particular issue, from the school principal on up to the president of the United States. Write or call whenever you react strongly to a proposed law. For example, let's say you see on TV that Congress plans to vote next week whether to cut funding for victims of domestic violence. You might want to tell your representatives what you think.

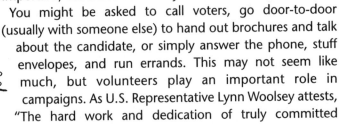

If you don't know your representatives' names, there are various ways to find out. Depending on the level of office, try calling the mayor's office or checking the government (blue) pages of the telephone book, or ask an adult who might know.

If you want to contact your representative or senators, you just need their names.

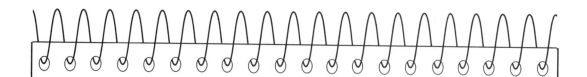

Then you can write to them in Washington:

Representative
The Honorable [first and last name]
House of Representatives
Washington, DC 20515

Senator
The Honorable [first and last name]
United States Senate
Washington, DC 20510

You can write to the president at the White House, Washington, DC 20500.

What do you say in a letter to a senator? How do you tell a representative you like or don't like something? It's pretty easy. Here are a few guidelines from *The Kid's Guide to Social Action:*

✿ When is the best time to write to a legislator? In December, which is the month before the new legislative session begins, so she'll have more time to read your letter.

✿ Include your return address so the legislator can write back.

✿ In your first sentence, state the purpose of your letter. If you're writing about a certain bill, mention its number and name.

✿ Address only one issue per letter.

✿ Keep your letter as short as possible—a few paragraphs at the most (just enough to get your point across).

✿ You can disagree with a public official, but do it in a polite way. Never be rude or threatening.

✿ Be complimentary if possible—mention something good the official has done. This could make her more receptive to hearing your complaint or suggestion.

✿ You don't need to apologize for taking the official's time. That's part of her job.

✿ If for some reason you write to a legislator other than the one who represents your district, send a copy of the letter to your representative. This is considered good manners, and your representative may want to help.

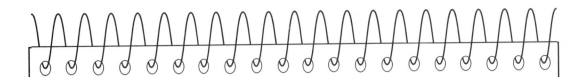

BE A LEADER

The editors of *The Information Please Women's Sourcebook* gave fourth-grade girls a list of fifty careers and asked them to select their favorites. Top choice: United States senator. If this includes you, start finding out if a leadership role would be appropriate for you. The sooner you get started, the better equipped you'll be to make things happen in the future, whether you want to be student body president in high school, a member of the city council, or president of the country in the year 2050.

If you think you'd make a good lawmaker, try playing the part of senator or representative in a model legislature. Many states have programs in which teens debate bills and pass laws, often in the state capitol building while the legislature is in recess. To find out if your state has a model program, call your state legislature. You can also contact Girls State, which teaches high school girls firsthand how the government works, at 777 No. Meridian St., Indianapolis, IN 46204; (317) 635-6291; or the Junior Statesmen, which has a summer program for kids ages fourteen to eighteen, at 60 East Third Ave., Suite 320, San Mateo, CA 94401-4032; (415) 347-1600.

"Somewhere out in this audience may even be someone who will one day follow in my footsteps and preside over the White House as the president's spouse. I wish *him* well."
—*Barbara Bush, during a commencement speech at Wellesley College*

A WOMAN'S PLACE IS . . . ON THE BALLOT

Test your knowledge of women in government. Make a copy, or write your responses on a separate sheet of paper, then check them against the answers on the next page.

1. Of the 100 senators and 435 representatives in Congress in 1997, how many were women?
   a. 11
   b. 28
   c. 60
   d. 100

2. How many minority women have ever served as members of Congress?
   a. 3
   b. 23
   c. 58
   d. 101

3. In 1997, only two women served as governor in the U.S.: Christine Todd Whitman of New Jersey, and Jeanne Shaheen of New Hampshire. Including them, how many women have ever been U.S. governors?
   a. 14
   b. 24
   c. 50
   d. 66

4. In 1997, what percentage of state legislators were women?
   a. 8 percent
   b. 21 percent
   c. 50 percent
   d. 67 percent

5. 1992 was called "The Year of the Woman." Why?
   a. 1991 was "The Year of the Man."
   b. A woman won the lottery.
   c. Lots of women were elected.
   d. Why *not?*

6. The country with the highest percentage of women in its main legislative assembly is:
   a. Norway
   b. Spain
   c. Sweden
   d. France

A Girl's Place Is in the House

by Amanda Keller, thirteen

Bethesda, Maryland

My cousin, Lisa, who is into politics, has always wanted me to be a politician. But to me, the whole government process seemed too complicated. I hardly knew there *was* a House of Representatives or a Senate, much less what they did. I basically thought the president did everything. So Lisa arranged for me to hang around with Representative Anna Eschoo on Take Our Daughters to Work Day.

When I got to Anna's office in Washington, one of her assistants showed me how things worked. Then Anna had a meeting, and I watched from where the public sits. Afterward, she invited me to go down on the floor, where the representatives were. And then she had to go up in the speaker's chair, so I went, too! It was pretty cool. She talked about the assets that had been frozen during the Persian Gulf War. I really enjoyed it, and it was good to see how everything worked.

That was my one big experience with government, and it made me see that there's more to politics than just the presidency. Being on the floor and seeing what Anna did made me realize that I could do it, too, and use the position to have an impact on women's rights. It inspired me to get into politics—in fact, it made me want to maybe go a step *higher,* to something even more exciting, like running for the Senate or the vice presidency.

For More Information

Breaking Barriers: The Feminist Revolution from Susan B. Anthony to Margaret Sanger to Betty Freidan, by Jules Archer (Viking, 1991). The inspiring stories of three activists' productive lives.

The Women's Movement, by Facts on File (Facts of File, 1995). The history of the fight for gender equality.

Is There a Woman in the House . . . or Senate? by Bryna J. Fireside (Whitman, 1993). Biographies of congresswomen throughout history. Grades six to ten.

It's Our World, Too! Stories of Young People Who Are Making a Difference, by Phillip Hoose (Little, Brown, 1993). Stories about activists and guidelines for making change happen.

Girls and Young Women Leading the Way, by Frances A. Karnes and Suzanne M. Bean (Free Spirit, 1993). Profiles twenty girls and young women who are doing inspiring projects in their schools and communities. Age eleven and up.

Careers for Women in Politics, by Richard S. and Mary Price Lee (Rosen Publishing Group, 1989). A primer on job opportunities in government. Grades seven to twelve.

Women of the U.S. Congress, by Isobel V. Morin (Oliver Press, 1994). Profiles seven women congressional representatives. Grades five to ten.

Women Win the Vote, by Betsy Covington Smith (Silver Burdett, 1989). Covers the history of women in the U.S. from 1620 to the present. Grades five to eight.

The Day Women Got the Vote, by George Sullivan (Scholastic, 1994). The story of women's struggle for voting rights. Grades four to seven.

"Women Win the Vote Gazette," by the National Women's History Project. A sixteen-page newspaper edition about the women's suffrage movement. National Women's History Project, 7738 Bell Rd., Windsor, CA 95492-8518; (707) 838-6000.

"Someday a Woman Will Be President!" T-shirts, available from Equilibrium, 1836 Ashley River Rd., Charleston, SC 29407; (803) 766-2232.

Girl Scouts, 1025 Connecticut Ave. NW, #309, Washington, DC 20036; (202) 659-3780. Sponsors projects that teach girls ages five to nineteen about civic responsibility.

Chapter 12
Spread the Word

"Peace on Earth, goodwill to men."

What is wrong with that phrase?

You guessed it: There's gender bias in it. The English language has traditionally used masculine nouns and pronouns to describe groups that also include girls and women. A more accurate ending for that sentence would be "Peace on Earth, goodwill to *all*."

This is not a big deal, you're probably saying. After all, everyone knows that the word *men* in that sentence is supposed to mean "men and women." And that if you say *he*, you really mean "he or she." Right?

Well, yes and no. Language makes people create pictures in their minds. And studies show that male-centered language makes children picture *just males,* the same way that words such as *women* make them picture *just females.* Think about it. If the word *man* really refers to both sexes, why do words or phrases such as *cameraman* and *Every man for himself* not seem to apply to women? Supposedly generic words such as *he* and *man* make women and girls seem insignificant and excluded, and they can affect women's lives in real ways. For example, researchers in one study found that when sexist pronouns were used in classified ads for jobs, women were less inclined to answer the ads. And even when sexist language isn't causing these kinds of problems, it's still annoying. "My science book talks about how *man* evolved," says Bridget Shanahan, thirteen, of Mokena, Illinois. "I don't think that's fair. I mean, didn't women evolve, too?"

Our language is biased in other ways as well. Women have traditionally been labeled by their marital status (*Miss* or *Mrs.*, which stands for "mistress of" her husband). This has placed unnecessary emphasis on women's marital status—while men haven't had to dis-

Old wives' tale

Chick
fox
broad
BABE
old maid

It's time to take out the trash!

close their status (they've all been *Mr.* whether single or married). In the 1970s, women's rights supporters came up with the title *Ms.* as a female equivalent to *Mr.*, but this still often seems to convey that a woman is single. Other subtle biases show up in our vocabulary. For example, hundreds of female words have negative connotations, such as *sissy,* which is derived from *sister,* and sexual connotations, such as *slut,* but there are relatively few such negative male terms. Another example of bias is the way women professionals are distinguished from men by the addition of trivializing beginnings or endings, as in *lady doctor,* as opposed to just *doctor,* and *empress* as opposed to *emperor.* Yet another, subtle form of bias is word order that consistently favors males, as in *boys and girls.*

People often perpetuate this type of bias without even realizing it. According to one study, preschool teachers used the pronouns *he* and *his* three times more often than *she* and *hers* when referring to animals that hadn't been defined as male or female. In some cases, it goes deeper than the language used, to basic patterns of thinking. In another study, participants were read a story that contained no gender bias and then asked about the mental pictures they formed. The females pictured men and women equally, but the males pictured men almost twice as often.

However, the language *is* still evolving, and its words are determined by the people who speak it. The younger generation is particularly influential—women and girls can do a lot to change speech habits. Certain new words and ways of using words may sound strange to you now, but when they were introduced, so did a lot of other "politically correct" words and phrases that now roll off our tongues, such as *gender neutral, people of color, significant other,* and *physically challenged.* Some changes are already so widely accepted that they're now in the dictionary, such as *herstory.* If enough girls and women use language that affirms our competence and importance, the new terms will become permanent, and we'll create a more positive, realistic picture of the population.

Using nonsexist language shows respect for women working in traditionally male jobs, such as the three police officers pictured here.

Things to Do

The best way to get rid of sexist language is to just stop using it. There are all kinds of ways to express the fact that girls and women are included, starting with replacing noninclusive words. Some common biased words and phrases with their accepted replacements are listed below. You can check *Elements of Nonsexist Usage: A Guide to Inclusive Spoken and Written English*, by Val Dumond (Prentice Hall, 1990), for more ideas.

Problem word or phrase	Acceptable substitute
actress	actor
suffragette	suffragist
forefathers	ancestors
waitress	waiter, waitperson
landlord	building owner
majorette	major
mailman	letter carrier
chairman	chairperson
policeman	police officer
fireman	firefighter
salesman	sales representative, salesperson
spokesman	spokesperson
stewardess	flight attendant
workmanship	artisanship
girl*	woman
lady**	woman
The gopher is digging his hole.	The gopher is digging its hole.
Mike is the best man for the job.	Mike is the best person for the job.
(In a letter) Dear Sirs, Gentlemen	To Whom It May Concern, Dear (name of person), Dear (name of organization), Greetings, Hello

---

* The word *girl* is often used to refer to women, implying immaturity. The technical definition of a girl is a female under age fifteen or so.

** The term *lady* connotes a weak, frilly person, as opposed to a strong, capable one.

Pay special attention to how you use pronouns, and try to stay gender neutral. Let's say you're writing a story about otters; instead of using *his* and *him* for all the animals, make some of them female and some male. If you would normally say something like "Every kid for himself," add "or herself." If you find that it's too awkward to repeatedly say *his or her,* alternate the pronouns. In a report about pet care, for example, you could refer to the owner as *she* in one paragraph, *he* in the next, and so on.

TEST A THEORY

Do an experiment to see if the language experts are right about how people form mental pictures. Compile a list of sexist words and phrases you've read or heard in conversations. When you've got about half a page, write a one-page story (fiction or nonfiction) that weaves the biased terms into your plot. Then write the same story, substituting gender-neutral words and phrases for the sexist ones. When you've finished, read each story to a different girl and see if the one who heard the biased story pictured more males than the one who heard the gender-neutral story did. Repeat this with two more friends if you like. Then let all of them in on the results.

SPREAD THE WORD

Another reason to use nonbiased language is that it may help convince your friends, parents, and teachers that they should use it, too. If someone laughs at the idea of bias-free language or at a bias-free phrase you use, explain that studies show that language affects the way people picture things and that women and girls are currently excluded by many words. If it's a boy or man, ask him how he would feel if the pronoun *she* and the term *woman* were always used to describe both men and women. You may not convince everyone, but you'll make a valid point.

Linguistic Losers

Did you notice sexist lingo before you ever read this chapter? Here are some pet peeves of girls across the country.

"Why is it that when a woman doesn't get married, she is called an 'old maid,' and when a man doesn't get married, he is called an 'eligible bachelor'?"

    —LYDIA LEINSDORF, *New York*

"There is a bank in my area named Young Men's Savings and Loan. I think it's very sexist because women get loans, earn money, and use banks just like men do. The name should be Young People's Savings and Loan. I plan to write to them and tell them how sexist they are."

    —KEELEY MCGROARTY, *Pitman, New Jersey*

"How come in collegiate sports at the University of Texas, they call the women's team Lady Longhorns and the men's team is just Texas or University of Texas? Why not the UT women's team and the UT men's team?"

    —CHLOE MCCOY, *nine, Austin, Texas*

"A few days ago I had some Campbell's soup. On the back it said, 'This soup has what it takes to handle a hungry man.' I was so mad!"

    —SARA BETH BEHMERWOHLD, *nine, San Juan Capistrano, California*

"I have nothing against different types of music, but I have a little problem with rap music. Why do rappers call women mean, nasty names?"

    —ANNA FOLMAN, *Columbus, Ohio*

"All the construction signs say MEN AT WORK. And I saw women."

    —JERIANN MILLER, *eleven, Marshall, Minnesota*

—from *New Moon: The Magazine for Girls and Their Dreams*

"I'm an *actor;* I don't understand *actress*. You don't call doctors *doctoresses* or *doctorettes*; you call them *doctors*."

—*Whoopi Goldberg, actor*

Name: Lucy Stone

First woman to: publicly protest the name-change custom

Preceding events: In 1855, Henry Blackwell, the man Stone had
been dating, proposed to her. She accepted but decided not to
change her name, saying that it was "the symbol of my identity
and must not be lost." After the wedding she called herself "Mrs.
Stone." She also wrote a marriage agreement that said she and Henry
would be equal partners.

The Great Last-Name Debate

Why is it that when a woman gets married she changes her last name? Well, it's an ancient convention. In the past, women were considered their husbands' property, and they gave up their names to reflect that. American women are no longer considered property, but 98 percent of American brides still take their husbands' names.

However, the number of women who don't change their names—or who figure out another option—may be growing. Supporters of women's rights ask why a woman should give up the identity she's had all her life just because she gets married. Name changing also makes it difficult for people to track down old friends who have gotten "lost" because no one knows their married names.

What do modern women do when they get married? Some keep their maiden names.

Some couples hyphenate their two names to make a new one. Other couples think of a different name altogether. Some women acknowledge that the tradition is sexist, but for various reasons—like not wanting to burden their children with long, hyphenated last names—they go along with the custom. There are no "right" answers, and every woman must decide what to do.

One modern man recently decided to buck the name-change convention. Neil Popović and his wife had always thought the convention was sexist, so he tried to change his last name to hers (they decided to add his name as a second middle name). Neil had a tough time getting the people at the Department of Motor Vehicles and the Internal Revenue Service to change the name on his driver's license and tax records. But he thought it was well worth the effort, because it raised people's awareness of the outdated custom. "You see, even if taking my wife's name is just a tiny blip on the radar screen of social evolution, it is still a thought-provoking act," he wrote in Ms. magazine.

Chapter 13
Selling Us Short

"Buy our products!" That's what companies are trying to get you to do with their TV spots, billboards, radio jingles, and ads in magazines and newspapers. You probably notice which ads are funny, which are splashy, which are persuasive and which aren't, and which campaigns you like or dislike. But have you noticed that quite a few ads feature stereotypical images of girls and women?

In a recent study of print ads, 97 percent depicted women in a degrading way (as a "dumb blond," a victim, or a sex object, for example). Take a closer look at magazine ads: Do they show women with their heads cut off by the top of the page? This type of framing seems to suggest the idea that how a woman looks is more important than what she thinks. Are there

close-up shots of thighs, breasts, lips, legs, or hips? These images suggest that individual body elements are more important than the whole person. Many ads feature women in degrading poses—models who look scared, as if they have been abused or are about to be hit; adult women posing as if they are little girls or who are portrayed as sex objects.

TV commercials are no better. A few stellar exceptions stand out, such as Nike's 1996 Summer Olympics spots focused on

TRUE or FALSE?

Jane's whole future depends on clean brite.

girls' potential. But we're generally barraged with images of housewives cheerfully discussing cleaning or cooking products or unrealistically thin young women in bikinis flocking around beer-drinking men. In addition, 83 percent of TV commercial voice-overs are male, often even in ads for women's products that show only women.

One reason some ads are so stereotypical and degrading to women and girls is that they're aimed at men, with scenarios that men can supposedly relate to. According to the American Psychological Association (APA), which issued a report on TV advertising in 1992, TV tries to appeal to young, affluent (usually white) people (usually men) who have the money to buy sponsoring companies' products, and these people do not represent most TV viewers. On the other hand, some ads, like those for diet products and weight-loss services, are targeted to women and are just as degrading. Another factor is that advertisers know sex sells, so they often inject sexual themes into ads for products that are totally unrelated to sex (such as car parts).

The APA advocates a return to the philosophy of the Communications Act of 1934, which requires television to focus on what the public wants and needs and to provide more sources of funding for shows besides commercials. However, we're not likely to see drastic changes in the way women and girls are shown in ads unless enough consumers get advertisers' attention and protest their ads.

Don't Buy It

Advertising is powerful—so powerful that TV shows have even been designed to complement their time slot's ads. A key example is soap operas, daytime dramas that were supposedly created so advertisers for detergents could reach women who were at home during the day. And advertisers are just as interested in reaching girls and getting their business. According to the *Los Angeles Times,* the average teen girl has $2,800 a year to spend on personal items such as cosmetics, and this is one reason companies buy billions of dollars worth of ads in magazines such as *Teen* and on networks such as MTV.

Your opinion is valuable to advertisers, and if you aren't buying their products and their advertising is offending you, they want to know about it. According to Naomi Wolf in *Fire with Fire: The New Female Power and How to Use It,* "Women have such tremendous power as consumers that when a woman writes a letter to a magazine—objecting, for example, to some ad's portrayals of women—that letter is counted as representing *ten thousand readers.*" Chances are you won't be the only person reacting to a particular ad, and if the company hears enough women and girls saying the same

HOT! 24 hour new lipstick makes you more desirable

thing, it will respond. Some companies have stopped running offensive ads, while others have gone so far as to design new campaigns that portray women more realistically. So the next time you see ads you don't like, remember that you have the buying power to help change them!

Girls Go After the Ads

A group of sixth-, seventh-, and eighth-grade girls participating in a Girl Scouts–Illinois Crossroads program called Making Choices protested companies' sexist or degrading ads. The girls looked at magazines and pulled out ads they found offensive, then formed groups and wrote letters telling the companies why. They won an award from the Media Action Alliance for their efforts. Here are some of the ads they chose and what they wrote:

Company: *Lipton*
Product: *Tea*
Ad image: *Woman getting a massage*
Girls' response: *A woman's naked body should not be used to sell your product. What does this have to do with tea? Men also drink tea—why don't you show a naked man? We would like to see a clothed, professional woman in a powerful role promoting the product. We choose not to buy Lipton tea, and we are surprised that you would stoop to this level.*

Company: *Buffalo*
Product: *Shoes*
Ad image: *Young, scantily clad woman sitting on old man's lap in little-girl pose*
Girls' response: *We object to your ads showing women in sexual poses, especially the one of the young woman sitting on the old man's lap. We want to see women shown in a positive manner, standing up and projecting strong self-esteem. We want you to change your ads or we will tell our families and friends to not buy your products.*

Company: *Boucheron*
Product: *Perfume*
Ad image: *Nude woman from the back with her hands bound at the wrists*
Girls' response: *We object to your showing a naked woman with her hands tied behind her back. How about showing the product you are selling? We choose not to buy your product until you change your ads. We look forward to hearing from you.*

Company: *Pepe*
Product: *Jeans*
Ad image: *Couple lying on couch; woman looks like a mannequin*
Girls' response: *We don't like the way you show women in your ads in a disrespectful way. You show a man controlling a woman and a woman who doesn't seem to care what happens to her. We want to see the jeans! We also want to see all varieties of women . . . all shapes and sizes. Better role models are very important. If you don't change your ads, we won't buy your product. We also plan on telling our friends and families.*

For more information about this project, send a self-addressed, stamped envelope to Girl Scouts–Illinois Crossroads Council, Making Choices, 570 E. Higgins Rd., Elk Grove Village, IL 60007.

Things to Do

BE AN AD ACTIVIST

Now that you know the story on advertising, you're ready to spot and challenge the worst offenders. Next time you see a TV commercial or an ad in a magazine or newspaper that portrays women in a negative or stereotypical way, sound off to the advertiser (call 1-800-555-1212 to get its 800 number), the TV station running it (see page 88 for the addresses of the networks), or the magazine. If you find an ad that portrays women in a *positive* way, you can also let the organization know you appreciate its efforts. The company may decide to continue running woman- and girl-positive ads if it knows they're being well received.

You can also send offensive ads to the editors of *Ms.* magazine, who feature the most sexist ads they receive on the magazine's back cover each month. Write down the date and name of the publication each ad came from, along with your name and address, and send it to: "No Comment," *Ms.* Magazine, 135 West 50th St., 16th Floor, New York, NY 10020.

ORGANIZE A GIRLCOTT

A boycott is a protest against a company whose policies or products are offensive or unfair. You might choose to boycott a company because it promotes unsafe products for women or creates ads that promote racism or sexism. Boycotting means not buying the company's products, telling the company why you aren't, and perhaps most important, trying to get other people to join the protest. If enough people do, the company will start feeling the heat and possibly do something to appease the boycotters and avoid bad publicity. For example, for a period beginning in 1977, activists boycotted the Nestle Corporation because it was promoting its infant formula in third-world countries. Activists argued that the use of formula was more dangerous than breast feeding because the water in many third-world areas is contaminated, and mixing it with infant formula could endanger babies' lives. The boycott did not have an effect on Nestle's sales and profits, but it did raise the company's awareness and cause the World Health Organization to set guidelines for advertising infant formula.

Why not organize a *"girl*cott*"* against a product that offends you? The more

people you can rally to your cause, the better. One way to recruit people is to create a flyer. Describe why you are boycotting the company and explain how others can help. List the company's products and include the name of its president or chief executive officer, along with the company and telephone number. Then hand out the flyer at school or community events. You might even want to stage a boycott as a class project.

Another alternative is to join an already existing boycott started by Media Watch, a membership group that protests sexist and degrading ads. It publishes a newsletter called "Action Agenda" (best for older girls) that describes ads and includes prewritten postcards addressed to companies. You can simply add your own comments to the cards, sign them, and drop them in the mail. Or you can use them as the basis for original letters or postcards, which will have even more impact. The newsletter also keeps readers posted about how the companies respond to these protests. See page 114 for subscription details.

Truths About Advertising

by Susan Gillette

Chicago

When I started as an advertising copywriter in the 1970s, most ads did not directly address women unless they were for products marketed exclusively to women, such as beauty, cleaning, and sanitary products. But instinctually I felt that women could be approached directly about a wide range of products. After I read research reports about how many women were purchasing their own cars, my art director, Lynn Crosswaite, and I tried to convince our client, STP, to run a print campaign in women's magazines touting its motor oil as a "not-so-feminine protection product." We positioned STP as something that could help women protect the sizable investments they make in their cars.

STP never ran that ad, but through the years we convinced many clients with products that traditionally were marketed to men, such as beer, cameras, and cars, to talk directly to women in their ads.

I helped persuade our beer client, Anheuser-Busch, to run a women's print campaign for Michelob Light beer. It used headlines in the style of the blurbs on the front of women's magazines, which say things like "Thinner thighs in 10 days" and "Make over your entire body." The ads poked fun at the fact that women's magazines feed into women's insecurities and made the point: "Hey, relax. You're OK. You don't need improving, but if you want to improve your beer, buy ours!" We were afraid magazines like *Glamour* and *Cosmopolitan* wouldn't run the ads because they made fun of the magazines, but they loved them. I guess that proves the female magazine editors had a good sense of humor!

Ten years ago, we had actor Felicia Rashad in a commercial for Yoplait saying she was eating yogurt so she could fit into a bikini. Today we show real women who are committed to a regime of exercising and healthy eating, and we encourage other women to include Yoplait in their diet by saying, "Do it for you! Don't do it so you can fit into a stereotype of beauty (or a bikini!) Do it for your health and well-being."

Advertising to women has come a long way in the twenty years since I started in the business. It's changed for the better, and the women working in the business have helped make that happen.

Susan Gillette was president of the advertising agency DDB Needham/Chicago for three years.

★★★ GOOD NEWS ★★★

Since 1982, the number of women working in ad agencies has increased 45 percent, and many of these women are becoming senior executives. Women's rights advocates hope this will translate into less sexist advertising.

Girls' Gripes

"In TV commercials for board games, there aren't enough girls playing, and boys always win. Commercials for dolls have all girls, and ones for G.I. Joes have all boys. I don't like that, because girls can play with G.I. Joes and boys can play with dolls!"

—ELANA MINGO, *ten, Alameda, California*

"Sometimes I think people who make commercials think it's still 1940. In commercials for cold medicine, the mom always gives the medicine to the kid who's sick. She stays home if someone's sick, and you never see a commercial with the father staying home. It's not like that at my house—my dad stays home with us half the time."

—SARAH HORNUNG, *thirteen, Haddam, Connecticut*

"Practically all the beer commercials show sexy-looking women wearing bathing suits. What do models in bathing suits have to do with beer? They never show men in revealing bathing suits."

—MOLLIE STRAFF, *thirteen, Philadelphia*

"My favorite radio station plays this one ad for a nightclub. The announcer says to come and see "the goddesses of swimwear." He says, "Unbelievable! You'll say you've never seen so many hot mamas!" and you can hear guys whistling in the background. I don't like the fact that this is accepted by our society. Girls, we do not have to take this!"

—ERICA KRUMM, *twelve, Savage, Minnesota*

"In most commercials for makeup and other beauty products, the announcer isn't even a woman—it's a man. I would like to see more commercials in which the woman wearing or using the product is the one to promote it."

—LAUREN WALES, *thirteen, Mason, Ohio*

For More Information

Media Watch, P.O. Box 618, Santa Cruz, CA 95061-0618; (408) 423-6355. Cost: fifteen to twenty dollars for a year (or check the local library; some libraries subscribe). This organization publishes a newsletter on sexism in advertising and the media in general (it also calls attention to nonsexist ads). It also has a video called *Warning: The Media May Be Hazardous to Your Health* (grade seven and up).

Chapter 14
Creative Differences

When you think of famous sculptors, painters, composers, novelists, dancers, playwrights, and poets, who comes to mind? There's Michelangelo, Monet, Beethoven, Dickens, Shakespeare, Homer, Frost, Whitman, Wordsworth...

These brilliant male artists have shaped our culture through the ages, but according to history books, there have been few women of the same caliber. Not for lack of talent: During the eras in which these artists lived, women were expected to focus on domestic work, so most didn't have time to pursue an interest in the arts. In addition, the women who *did* have time weren't given the same encouragement or allowed the same level of education as men. For example, only men were invited to be in the prestigious art guilds and get the high-level training that often led to their success. To top it off, writers of history books have not given full credit to the women artists who did succeed despite the odds.

The one area of the arts in which women have been historically less limited is writing, partly because

women could write at home between household chores. But even writing was considered an "unfeminine" pursuit, and female authors weren't taken seriously, which is why many of them used male pen names. The famous novelist George Eliot, for example, was really a woman named Mary Ann Evans.

Fortunately women writers no longer have to hide behind pen names, and today there are thousands of women in all areas of the arts. What's more, not only are more women creating art, but since the 1970s, especially, they have been producing well-received work with female-affirming themes. For example, Judy Chicago has received widespread recognition for her paintings that allude to women's bodies. Poet Maya Angelou, whose work affirms the power and strength of women, was chosen to read at President Bill Clinton's 1993 inauguration, and filmmaker Christine Choy has won awards for movies she has made about battered women, women in prison, and child care. A group of musicians has formed the Bay Area Women's Philharmonic, the only professional all-female orchestra in the country, which plays music by outstanding female composers. And quilt artist Faith Ringgold has created work that celebrates African-American women and girls, who are not being represented in most art museums.

Activists are also working to promote the inclusion of more women in the arts. Perhaps the best known: a group of anonymous women artists called the Guerrilla Girls. It points out that 51 percent of American artists today are women but an estimated 95 percent of the art in our museums is by men and that female artists earn a third as much as male artists. The group's posters, which target sexism, racism, and censorship, have appeared at random all over New York City. One poster, headed "Advantages of Being a Woman Artist," lists such ironic "advantages" as "working without the pressure of success." The group also uses humor in other ways to get its message across; for instance, the members make public appearances wearing gorilla masks.

If you want to be an artist, musician, dancer, actor, producer, director, or writer, hold on to that dream! You may have a powerful message for the world. And who knows? You could end up following in the footsteps of a woman like photographer Annie Liebovitz, choreographer Martha Graham, or writer Virginia Woolf—or blazing a new trail all your own.

"For a long time, the only time I felt beautiful—in the sense of being complete as a woman, as a human being, and even female—was when I was singing."
—*Leontyne Price, opera singer*

116

Character Flaws

by Marie G. Lee

New York

Karl Jacoby

When I was in Korea for the summer, my twelve-year-old cousin fell so in love with the Disney movie *The Little Mermaid* that she bought an English-language copy of the book.

I read the book to her at least once a week. The story started to annoy me because I liked the original Hans Christian Andersen version better: The Little Mermaid foolishly pursues a prince and ends up turning into sea foam. In the Disney version, she ends up *marrying* the prince.

But what really began to annoy me was how all the "good" characters were male: the father, the prince, the lobster, etc. The "bad" character was the sea witch, who schemes to steal the Little Mermaid's lovely voice.

That made me think about the female characters in fairy tale movies from my own childhood. For instance, why is the villain in *Snow White* an evil, jealous mother (and the prince and the elves are all male and good)? In *101 Dalmations*, the villain is Cruella, who wants to kill Dalmatian puppies just so she can have a fur coat to match her hair. And let's not forget *Cinderella,* with its record-breaking four evil female characters.

Almost everyone grows up seeing one if not all of the movies mentioned here, and this points out a need to look at books and movies to examine how our society portrays and regards women. Too often we are ready to accept whatever is shown to us, even when we know better. For me, it took reading this story to my cousin over and over again to see what was wrong with it. I know that as a writer I will try to include many positive female characters inspired by the *real* women—my mother, my sister, my aunt, my friends—in my life.

Marie G. Lee has written several fiction books for teens, including Finding My Voice *and* If It Hadn't Been for Yoon Jun.

Leader of the Band

by JoAnn Falletta

San Francisco

My music studies began when I was seven years old. I played guitar, piano, and cello. About the time I was twelve, my parents started taking me to concerts and I fell in love with the orchestra. I had never experienced anything like that, seeing a group of people working together to create something so special. It was then that I decided I wanted to be able to shape the interpretation of that magnificent instrument, the symphony orchestra.

I first went to the conservatory when I was eighteen. I spent an entire year before I was permitted to major in conducting because the college administrators said no woman had ever succeeded in the field. They didn't want to encourage me to be a conductor because they could not see any chance of my succeeding in that exclusively male domain. It took me a year to convince them. Their resistance surprised me. I just kept doing as well as I could in my courses and telling them that I was interested and that I recognized it had never been done. I was lucky when a new teacher came to the school who was a little younger and more understanding about the possibilities for women.

Today the major symphonies, particularly the older musicians and older board members, still have some reservations about a young American woman conductor. We will change that attitude through professionalism and hard work. I have three orchestras and I conduct about 120 concerts a year. I could never have predicted this ten years ago. But I always felt that somehow I would make it because I knew I wanted it so much. I had the good fortune to be invited as a guest conductor all over the United States, Europe, and Asia.

Of course, there are disappointments and difficulties, but the moments of magic more than make up for them. To hear a Mozart symphony take shape in your hands, to see an orchestra work with all its heart and talent toward the creation of something beautiful, to feel that together we have moved and uplifted our audience beyond the cares and troubles of their everyday lives—all this makes working as a conductor the realization of my most cherished dream.

JoAnn Falletta (pictured below) is music director and conductor of the Virginia Symphony and the Long Beach Symphony. She also works with the San Francisco–based Women's Philharmonic.

Things to Do

LEARN ABOUT WOMEN IN THE ARTS

Are you wondering what subject to tackle for that next "free-choice" class assignment? How about researching and reporting on a woman in the arts? Many people are uninformed about women artists—past or present—and would probably enjoy learning about them. You might choose one woman and do an in-depth report, or profile several women from a particular era or field. Here are a few books to get you started:

Letter to the World: The Life and Dances of Martha Graham, by Trudy Garfunkel (Little, Brown, 1995).

The Norton Anthology of Literature by Women, edited by Sandra M. Gilbert and Susan Gubar (Norton, 1985). Best for older girls, grade nine and up.

Visions: Stories about Women Artists, by Leslie Sills (Whitman, 1993).

Focus: Five Women Photographers, by Sylvia Wolf (Whitman, 1994).

A Young Painter: The Life and Paintings of Wang Yani, China's Extraordinary Young Artist, by Zheng Zhensun and Alice Low (Scholastic, 1991).

If you'd just like to learn more about women in the arts for your own sake, break out the playing cards: The National Women's History Project distributes two card games that are played like Go Fish or Rummy, using cards that feature various women artists. To order the games "Poets and Writers" or "Composers" (as well as several other non-art-related games), contact the organization at 7738 Bell Rd., Windsor, CA 95492-8518; (707) 838-6000.

WRITE A FAIRY TALE

Rapunzel, Cinderella, Sleeping Beauty . . . you probably remember these childhood fairy tales well. Although they could never happen in real life, people have loved them for generations. But unfortunately, most traditional fairy tales do not have good role models for women. In each of these three mentioned, for example, a prince is necessary for the heroine to overcome her problems. Just think what wonderful things might have happened if these women had been able to save themselves!

If you like to write, craft your own fairy tale that features *you* as the heroine. This can be more inspiring than reading something by the Brothers Grimm, because you create and control the story. Your fairy tale can have any plot you want. It doesn't have to be realistic, since magic and make-believe are what fairy tales are all about. The format should go something like this: Faced with a difficult situation, you must find your way through it. You go on some kind of adventure, meeting up with allies who help you overcome various obstacles. You may encounter enemies and confront darkness and fear, but ultimately you emerge victorious.

So get out a pen and paper and start imagining. If you could do anything you wanted in the world, what would it be? What challenges would you face, and what rewards would you reap?

When you've finished writing your fairy tale, read it to a female friend (you could both do this exercise and then share your stories). Or trade stories with a pen pal: contact the Young People's Project, which matches up teen girls so they can compare and comment on each other's writing. The address: International Women's Writing Guild, P.O. Box 810, Gracie Station, New York, NY 10028; (212) 737-7536.

HAVE A PAINTING PARTY

A mural is a large work of art that usually conveys a particular idea or theme. It may be painted on paper or on a wall, by one artist or by many. Why not organize a group of girls to paint a mural that honors girls and women?

For starters, invite several girls whom you think would enjoy the project to participate. They don't have to be fantastic artists, but they should enjoy painting. When you've got five or six people, get together and discuss what you want the mural to communicate. For example, your theme could be female contributions in the arts, women in leadership roles in general, or Greek goddesses.

Ask everyone to chip in for the art supplies. Go to an art store and buy a roll of butcher paper or heavy-weight drawing paper, enough acrylic paint to complete your design, pencils, wide masking tape (to secure the mural while you're working on it), and paintbrushes. Convert a few tin cans or plastic containers into water containers. Tape the paper on a smooth wall in someone's house or garage, at a park, or in some other convenient place. Sketch the images you want to paint, and then spend the day filling them in. When you've finished, look for places to display the work (such as at a kids' art show), or see if your school has a good place for it.

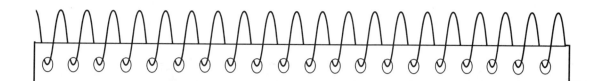

For More Information

Evening the Score: Women in Music and the Legacy of Frederique Petrides, by Jan Bell Groh (University of Arkansas Press, 1991). A history of women in music and the Belgian twentieth-century conductor Frederique Petrides. Best for girls fifteen and up.

Ladyslipper, P.O. Box 3124, Durham, NC 27715; (919) 683-1570. Distributes a catalog of various types of music by female musicians and composers.

National Museum of Women in the Arts, Education Department, 1250 New York Ave. NW, Washington, DC 20005; (202) 783-5000. This organization works to promote women in the arts. For a free sample copy of "ScoutsAbout," its Girl Scout newsletter (published twice a year) about exhibitions and projects at the museum, send a self-addressed, stamped envelope with fifty-five cents postage. Also available: a catalog of books, posters, and games.

Writes of Passage USA Inc., 817 Broadway, 6th Floor, New York, NY 10003; (212) 473-7564; http://www.writes.org. Publishes stories and poems by young adults.

lawyer

scientist

Chapter 15
Working Woman

Take a guess: What is generally considered the most important goal of women's rights advocates?

The answer: economic equity. There's a fundamental connection between earning your own money and being able to take care of yourself. Having a job gives you independence and freedom to live as you choose. What's more, a career can challenge you intellectually and creatively, help you learn new skills, raise your self-esteem, give you a sense of purpose, improve your social life, allow you to travel, and be a lot of fun!

doctor

Women on the Job

In the United States, the majority of women work outside the home. Like most men, they have rent or mortgages to pay, food and clothes to buy, and often families to support. Many women work full-time, while others work part-time so they can devote more attention to their families. Some women work solely at home, keeping the household running and taking care of their children.

pilot

Times have changed a great deal since a few decades ago, when married women were expected to be housewives while their husbands worked, when it was considered unusual for married women to even have jobs, and when companies and the government were allowed to discriminate against women in hiring and promotion. This change has happened partly because women have pushed for equal employment opportunities and partly for economic reasons. It used to be that a family could live on the man's income alone, but now, because of inflation, two incomes are often needed to make ends meet. According to a 1994 *New York Times* and CBS News poll, only 7 percent of girls ages thirteen to seventeen expect that they would stay home after getting married.

writer

However, there is still a debate going on in this country about women and work. Some people still believe the old saying "A woman's place is in the home" and argue that when mothers work, their children suffer. Some men don't like having to compete with women at work, and some husbands want their wives to manage the household. Supporters of women's rights counter that women need and deserve to work just as much as men and that when they do, their families and the economy benefit. Many parents argue that putting children in day care while their mothers work has no ill effects on their personal development and that a mother who works outside the home is a good role model for her children. And women point out that when they contribute actual income to their families—as opposed to doing the undervalued job of being a homemaker—they feel a stronger sense of equality with their spouses. Everyone has an opinion about this issue, and families handle it in different ways.

Pay Equity

Women also face challenges in the workplace itself. One big issue is women's earning power. On the average, American women ages twenty-five to thirty-four earn eighty-three cents for every dollar men earn (for *all* working women, it's closer to seventy-two cents to the dollar). In addition, jobs that have historically been held mainly by women, such as receptionist or cosmetologist, pay less than comparable jobs (in other words, those requiring similar skill levels) held mainly by men, such as maintenance worker or electrician. And according to a 1994 report by the federal government, women are "segregated in low-paying, traditionally female jobs in clerical, sales, and service occupations."

Men have supposedly been paid more in the past because of the assumption that they had families to support. This rationale never made much sense because women also had families to support. But it's especially unfair now because a large number of women are supporting families (many as single mothers), and their income is critical. And even if women *don't* support a family or are the second source of income for their household, they should still receive equal pay, just as men who don't support a family do.

The Glass Ceiling

Women haven't had the same opportunities as men to move into leadership positions at work. At least ninety-five percent of all top executive jobs in America's major companies are still held by men, thanks to the "glass ceiling," an invisible barrier of sex discrimination that keeps women from moving up. In addition, companies are often structured so that certain jobs that are typically held by women, such as those in public relations or human resources, don't naturally lead to top management.

Why are barriers for women at work so hard to crack? Eighty-one percent of *Fortune* 500 chief executive officers surveyed in 1990 agreed that sexist stereotypes and preconceptions are one of the main reasons. Affirmative action, a national policy giving women and minorities an equal chance of being hired and promoted, was adopted in 1961, but in 1995 it was phased out, in part because of complaints that it was fostering "reverse discrimination" against white males. However, as current top male executives get ready to retire, many women are waiting to replace them, so things could still improve.

The issue of women and work obviously has many facets, and you need to know how all of them can affect you. But right now you mainly need to realize that you have options when it comes to working and/or raising a family.

★★★ GOOD NEWS ★★★

Male boss or female boss—which is better? The traditional assumed answer has always been male (since "women are too emotional"), but a survey reported in 1996 by the Foundation for Future Leadership says the opposite. The study, involving more than six thousand people working at companies of all sizes, found that in general, women managers delegate work more often, communicate, organize, and plan more effectively, and are more flexible than men.

Things to Do

KEEP YOUR OPTIONS OPEN

Keeping in mind your own particular interests and abilities, one way to ensure that you earn what you're worth is to choose and be educated for a job that pays well. This isn't to say that you shouldn't consider working in traditionally "female" fields; it's just that it's smart to be open to *all* of the possibilities for fulfilling work.

You can maximize your career options by waiting until you graduate from college (or high school if you're not going on for further schooling) to have children. One million teen girls get pregnant each year, limiting their ability to continue their education and get a high-paying job. "Between the ages of fourteen and twenty, you make critical decisions that can affect the course of your whole life—decisions about classes to take, career options, lifetime mates, and family timing," says Betty Shepperd, national coordinator of a program called Women Helping Girls With Choices. You should be able to make these choices without having to deal with being a parent.

EXPLORE YOUR OPTIONS

Ever since you learned to talk, people have probably been asking you, "What do you want to be when you grow up?" Maybe you've answered with something you've dreamed of being since you were little, like a gymnast or an astronaut. Maybe you've had a hard time answering this question because you have no idea. But this is a good time to start thinking about it and being open to all the possibilities. In a recent national survey of women, 79 percent said they like or love their jobs. What do you like to do? Your interests can translate into a career you'll enjoy. Keep in mind that today people often have a succession of careers throughout their lifetime, so you don't have to decide on just one career.

INTERVIEW WORKING WOMEN

Another way to get ideas about careers is to ask women to tell you about their jobs. (Of course you can also ask men, but it's good to get a woman's perspective.) This is called informational interviewing. If a specific job interests you, ask your family and friends if they know someone who does that type of work. If you don't have a particular job in mind, try interviewing your mother, then a friend, teacher, boss, or relative. Keep each interview short—fifteen minutes at most. The more interviews you do, the more interesting information you'll collect.

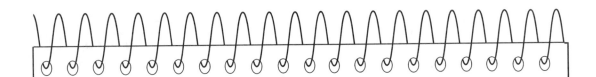

Here are some questions to ask each person:

1. What is your typical day like?

2. What skills do you use?

3. How did you start doing this?

4. What do you like most about your job?

5. What do you like least?

6. What obstacles have you encountered?

7. Are you interested in changing to another career? Why or why not?

8. In your profession, do you think women are treated the same as men?

9. If you had the choice, would you rather work at home than at an outside job?

10. If you could live your life again, what would you do differently in your career?

11. Do you have any advice for me about careers?

After each interview, send a brief thank-you note, letting the person know you appreciated her taking the time to talk to you. Mention something you learned from the interview and how it affected you. If she knows you found the interview useful, she may refer you to other people you can interview.

GO TO WORK!

One of the most valuable ways to expand your career knowledge is to go to work with an adult. You've probably heard of Take Our Daughters to Work Day, an event sponsored by the *Ms.* Foundation that takes place on the fourth Thursday in April each year. On that day, more than five million girls visit offices and work sites around the world, taking part in special demonstrations and observing their relatives and friends at work. Girls visit corporate offices, construction sites, government agencies, television stations, and factories. According to a recent poll, 84 percent of adults think the event is a positive experience for girls.

If you'd like to participate in Take Our Daughters to Work Day, here are some tips:

1. Ask an adult whose job interests you to take you to work. You may relate to the experience better if you choose a woman as your sponsor.

2. Tell your female friends about Take Our Daughters to Work Day, and find out if they are participating. If they aren't, invite them to come with you (that is, if it's OK with your sponsor) or suggest that they find someone who has a job that interests them.

3. Contact the *Ms.* Foundation to get a girls' Take Our Daughters to Work Day checklist and how-to tips, along with information for adults. The address is 120 Wall St., 33rd Floor, New York, NY 10005. Or call (800) 676-7780, or visit their Web site at http://www.ms.foundation.org/.

4. Be aware that there is some controversy about this event, as some parents of boys think that boys should be included. Some companies call the day Take Our Kids to Work Day. Advocates for the day say having boys go to work the same day defeats one of the main purposes of the event, which is to give girls a chance to explore work without having to compete with boys for attention or feel intimidated by them (see chapter 6, Class Acts, for information on how boys and girls behave together at school). Boys could have any other day of the year. If someone tells you it's not fair to exclude boys, acknowledge their right to that opinion, but if you believe in girls having their own day, stick to yours.

BECOME AN ENTREPRENEUR

Starting a business isn't what most people encourage teens to do, but more and more young women are discovering that being one's own boss has its advantages. More than eight million American women own businesses, and these companies generate more than two trillion dollars in sales. Entrepreneurs report that their lives are more meaningful than when they were employed by a company because they're doing something they believe in or because they're in charge. Self-employed people often have more flexible schedules since they determine when the work gets done. Finally, running a successful business can be far more profitable than working for someone else.

A group of girls in Carpinteria, California, has explored what it means to run its own enterprise. The girls, in conjunction with the local chapter of Girls Incorporated, started a T-shirt design company. Sonia Lopez, one group member who is now nineteen, reports that running the business made her want to be independent. Another member, Marisela Marchan, sixteen, says she now feels more confident doing things on her own. "It was hard for me to talk on the phone before, but now it's easy to call people and make marketing presentations," she says.

Another young woman who started her own business is Jennifer Davis, now eighteen, of Pacific Junction, Iowa, who rents machinery to construction workers. It hasn't always been easy, but she has discovered that she likes being in charge. "I'm learning that if I want something to get done the way I want, I have to do it myself," she says. "I think given my circumstances, I'm doing really well. And when I get paid, that's even more great—like 'Yes, I did it.' "

Do you have an idea for a business of your own? Enter it in the National Teen

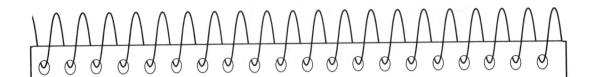

Business Plan Competition. To get a contest entry form, contact Lynn Karlson at An Income of Her Own, P.O. Box 987, Santa Barbara, CA 93102; (800) 350-2978; http://www.anincomeofherown.com. To enter, you'll need to write about your ideal business and how you would make it a success. Contest winners receive a business resource kit and a free trip to meet women business owners (locations vary). Past winners have gone on to start a mail-order clothing company for tall girls and a service that assigns odd jobs for the elderly to teen volunteers, among others. The contest sponsor also has other programs and distributes a board game in which players assume the roles of business partners (for age thirteen and up).

When I Grew Up

by Jody L. Rohlena

Red Bank, New Jersey

They didn't have Take Our Daughters to Work Day when I was growing up in a small town in Iowa, and my visions of what I could do when I grew up were rather limited. I used to watch adults doing what they do and try to imagine myself behind the desk, in front of the classroom, at the teller's window. My mother sometimes took me to the photography studio where she worked touching up photographs by hand. It looked like fun, but it wasn't my dream. My dad, a state trooper, used to take me and my friends for rides in his squad car. One time he locked a bunch of us in a holding cell in City Hall—trying to deter us from a life of crime, no doubt. But I didn't see a career in law enforcement for myself.

Ultimately, I grew up to be a magazine editor, among other things. As a young girl, I never knew such a job existed. That's the best part about Take Our Daughters to Work Day—firsthand knowledge of the previously unknown. When I worked at the magazine *New Woman,* we invited girls to observe how things worked on Take Our Daughters to Work Day. I saw myself in the face of each young potential editor. That's the reward for the adults: We can't help but revisit our own girlhoods, remembering what we wanted to be, thinking about what made us who we are today. Our goal is to help girls imagine that they, too, might one day edit a magazine, or run a corporation, or fly an airplane. It's true that one day a year won't shatter the glass ceiling or give women equal pay. But it will help girls to dream, to think with confidence and without limitation about the women they can become— what they can be when they grow up.

128

What I Did on Take Our Daughters to Work Day

by Jasmine J. Victoria, thirteen

New York

It all started when I met Carol Jenkins, a famous news anchor at Channel 4, at a town hall meeting for girls to inform people about Take Our Daughters to Work Day. I was covering the event as a reporter for *Children's Express*, a children's newswriting service. I asked Carol what her plans were for Take Our Daughters to Work Day, then mustered up the courage to ask if I could spend the day with her. I was so excited when she said yes.

Several girls came to the news station at NBC that day. We were given a tour and met many other reporters, producers, and camerapeople. We got to see what goes on behind the scenes and all the hard work that goes into putting together the evening news. We also met Jane Pauley and Katie Couric—see them on TV all the time!

Sometimes you look at people on TV and see them as superhuman; you don't think you can talk to them. If you see them in person, you just ask for their autograph. I found myself conversing with these people (OK, I did ask for their autographs as well). I gained a lot of confidence, and I learned there's nothing to be afraid of. As my mother always says, "They're not going to bite you." I learned a lot about the journalism world and specifically about the important jobs women hold at NBC. I hope to be a journalist someday, so this was a good experience for me.

At the end of the day, Carol asked us if anyone wanted to do a "stand-up," which is when you stand in front of the camera and give a brief recap of the story. Everyone else was too shy, so I volunteered. I was a little nervous because it was my first time. I wasn't sure if I should act like a real reporter and say, "From Channel 4 News, this is Jasmine Victoria." I gestured over to Carol, asking if it was OK that I'd said that, and she nodded. I thought I had messed up, but at the station they liked it and did not edit out my mistake. All my friends saw me on TV and thought it was funny.

Spending the day with an important woman like Carol Jenkins, who treated me like I was special, made me realize that girls should demand more respect in this world. I'm doing that now!

"The test for whether or not you can hold a job should not be the arrangement of your chromosomes."

—Bella Abzug, activist and author

Name: Grace Hopper

First woman (or male) to: develop a computer compiler and programming language

Preceding events: Born in 1906, Hopper showed signs of technical skills as a girl; one of her hobbies was taking apart mechanical items such as alarm clocks. After serving in the U.S. Navy as a computer programmer, she was hired by the Eckert-Mauchly Corporation. Seeking to eliminate the time-consuming programming task of repeatedly typing in certain commands, she invented the computer language COBOL. Dubbed the Mother of Computing, she died in 1992.

For More Information

Career Choices: A Guide for Teens and Young Adults, by Mindy Bingham and Sandy Stryker (Academic Innovations, 1990). A workbook with career exploration exercises. Grade eight and up.

Rosie the Riveter: Women Working on the Home Front in World War II, by Penny Colman (Crown, 1995). The story of how American women filled the shoes of working men during the Second World War.

Women & Work: In Their Own Words, edited by Maureen Michelson (New Sage Press, 1994). Stories about women's careers. Grade eight and up.

It's a Living: Career News for Girls, published by Ceel Publishing, 1643 Fitzgerald Lane, Alexandria, VA 22302; (703) 671-1835. Profiles women in a wide variety of jobs.

A Girl's World, by Laurie Hepburn. Video about career opportunities. Available from Laurie Hepburn Productions, 449 Main St., Ridgefield, CT 06877; (800) 275-9101. Kindergarten to ninth grade.

"Girls Can Do Anything" T-shirts, available from the Feminist Majority, 1600 Wilson Blvd., #801, Arlington, VA 22209; (703) 522-2214.

Conclusion: Secrets of Success

OK, you've read this book! Now what? You don't actually have to go out and *do* anything different. What matters is that you've increased your awareness and realized that you have options when you are faced with certain people, situations, and media messages. Of course, at some point you may want to put some of this book's principles into action. When you do, keep in mind a few practical suggestions.

Be Prepared

In a perfect world, girls and women would be on equal footing with boys and men in all regards. But as of the day this book went to press, they weren't. Some boys will always think girls aren't as good at sports, even if girls beat them hands down every time. Some women will always be resistant to changes in female roles even if they improve life for women. And some friends will never agree with you, even if your opinion makes perfect sense and you have statistics to back it up. People have their own convictions, and you're not going to be able to win them all over to your views. But has any of this stopped girls and women from speaking out on their own behalf and working for social change? Not for a minute.

Respect Others' Opinions

No two people think alike, and this includes activists. For instance, some women's rights supporters feel that men should not open doors for women because it subtly suggests that women need assistance. Others believe that opening a door is a polite gesture for *anyone*—male or female—to make. If you want to change someone's outlook on an issue, first try to "get in the person's shoes." Don't attack people's views or tell them they're wrong. People don't generally enjoy being around someone who's "on a soapbox" or ranting about an issue—it can make them feel judged and alienated. Instead, focus on raising awareness of issues by talking about how *you* feel. Other people will be more likely to be receptive to adopting new attitudes if they do not feel pressured or criticized.

Value Good Guys

Let's face it: Promoting women's rights might not make you a magnet for every boy at school. The concept of girls and women having power and using their brains can feel threatening to boys and men, as you know if you've ever stuck up for yourself and had a guy act like a jerk in response! Some guys might not ask you out, but if you've read this book and can identify with its principles, you probably wouldn't want to hang around with these boys anyway. There *are* desirable, attractive boys and men who'll like you as you are *and* respect you for your beliefs.

Be Patient

If you make an effort to stop gender bias in your own life or in society, you may not see quick results. Change takes time—each generation of girls and women slowly makes some progress. The more that girls get involved now, the closer we get to true equality.

Laugh a Little!

The issues in this book are important, no doubt. However, you can approach discussions with a light touch and still make your beliefs known. If there's any way you can laugh about an issue or make others laugh, you'll probably put people at ease and be more successful in communicating your ideas.

The Last Word

No matter how you present your thoughts and ideas to people, remember that they are important thoughts and ideas. You have unique and valuable observations and suggestions to contribute. Remember that you deserve every opportunity that any boy (or any other girl, for that matter) deserves. Last of all, remember that you can take charge of the issues that affect you and, in the process, set yourself up to live a rewarding, successful, and happy life.

I've had a great time writing this book for you. I hope you've enjoyed reading it, and that it's given you lots of useful new information. If you liked it, please share it with a friend, as helping others learn about the issues will strengthen your ability to make things happen.

Do you have any comments about the book or a story you would like to share? If so, I'd like to know in case I can incorporate it in any future editions of this book or in a new book. Please write me in care of Little, Brown, and Company, Children's Division, 3 Center Plaza, Boston, MA 02108, or send me E-mail at cate@deebest.com. I look forward to hearing from you!

Catherine Dee

Gender Inequity

It began long ago…
    it's always been so
      historically.

    From
    voting
     to
    working jobs
     to
    passing laws,

we've fought.

    But…
society still stands in our way.

It threatens to tear us apart,
    knock us down
      mistreat us
    and deprive us of our lawful rights.

This world plays rough.
    You *must* be prepared.
    That
is why we must teach our children

about inequity, both boys and girls.
    That
is the only way we can make it right.

We must correct our mistakes of the past.
    Forgive ourselves and each other and
    work together toward greater goals of
    equity among men and women
      boys and girls
    everyone.

It's going to be hard,
    but it will be worth it.

Maybe we can fix this world for generations to
    come.

    It only takes a strong will
      and an open heart.

We'll make it.

Just watch….

— Sarah Duff Harris, thirteen
Chapel Hill, North Carolina

133

Resources for Parents and Teachers

If you have a daughter or female students in the ten- to fifteen-year-old range, you're undoubtedly aware of the impact that gender bias in our culture has on girls. Maybe you've wished there were some basic, suitable educational material you could give girls to help them understand it.

This book is not an exhaustive guide to every issue, and it doesn't cover certain topics that seem more appropriate for older girls and young women or that other books already cover (such as health, sexuality, and general adolescent concerns). It explains women's issues in an upbeat, straightforward way that's meant to empower girls and give them a head start so they can respond constructively to challenges in the years ahead.

Of course, once girls begin learning about the issues, they may turn to you for additional guidance and perspective. Therefore, I've included this resource list, which features some key books, magazines, and organizations that address how to help girls.

Here's to raising a generation of girls who meet the challenges of being female with conviction, courage, and confidence!

Books

Mother-Daughter Choices, by Mindy Bingham, Lari Quinn, and William P. Sheehan (Advocacy Press, 1988).

Things Will Be Different for My Daughter: A Practical Guide to Building Her Self-Esteem, by Mindy Bingham and Sandy Stryker with Susan Allstetter Neufeldt (Penguin, 1995).

Beyond Dolls & Guns: 101 Ways to Help Children Avoid Gender Bias, by Susan H. Crawford (Heinemann, 1995).

Mother-Daughter Revolution, by Elizabeth Debold, Marie Wilson, and Idelisse Malavae (Addison-Wesley, 1993).

All That She Can Be: Helping Your Daughter Achieve Her Full Potential and Maintain Her Self-Esteem During the Critical Years of Adolescence, by Carol J. Eagle and Carol Colman (Simon & Schuster, 1993).

Raising a Daughter: Parents and the Awakening of a Healthy Woman, by Jeanne Elium and Don Elium (Celestial Arts, 1994).

Raising Strong Daughters, by Jeanette Gadeberg (Fairview Press, 1995).

No More Frogs to Kiss: 99 Ways to Give Economic Power to Girls, conceived by members of An Income of Her Own, edited by Joline Godfrey (HarperCollins, 1995).

What Parents Need to Know About Dating Violence, by Barrie Levy and Patricia O. Giggans (Seal Press, 1995).

How to Father a Successful Daughter, by Nicky Marone (Fawcett, 1989).

Creating the Nonsexist Classroom: A Multicultural Approach, by Theresa Mickey McCormick (Teachers College Press, 1994).

Gender Positive! A Teachers' and Librarians' Guide to Nonstereotyped Children's Literature, K–8 (McFarland & Company, 1993).

Schoolgirls: Young Women, Self-Esteem, and the Confidence Gap, by Peggy Orenstein (Doubleday, 1994).

Reviving Ophelia: Saving the Selves of Adolescent Girls, by Mary Pipher (Putnam, 1994).

Mother Journeys: Feminists Write about Mothering, edited by Maureen Reddy, Martha Roth, and Amy Sheldon (Spinsters Ink, 1994).

Celebrating Girls: Empowering and Nurturing Our Daughters, by Virginia Beane Rutter (Conari, 1996).

Lifting the Barriers: 600 Strategies That Really Work to Increase Girls' Participation in Science, by Jo Sanders. (Jo Sanders Publications, 1994). A book for educators. Available from the publisher, (206) 543-1847.

Why It's Great to Be a Girl, by Jacqueline Shannon (Warner, 1994).

A Sense of Self: Listening to Homeschooled Adolescent Girls, by Susannah Sheffer (Boynton/Cook, 1995).

How to Stop Sexual Harassment in Our Schools: A Handbook and Curriculum Guide for Administrators and Teachers, by Robert J. Shoop and Debra L. Edwards (Prentice Hall, 1994).

How to Encourage Girls in Math and Science, by Joan Skolnick, Carol Langbort, and Lucille Day (Prentice Hall, 1982).

Feminist Parenting: Struggles, Triumphs, and Comic Interludes, edited by Dena Taylor (Crossing Press, 1994).

The Scientist Within You: Experiments and Biographies of Distinguished Women in Science, by Rebecca L. Warren and Mary H. Thompson (ACI Publishing, 1996).

Gender Equity—Past, Present, and Future: A Resource Book for Working with Adolescents (1996). Available from Upper Midwest Women's History Center, c/o Hamline University, 1536 Hewitt Ave., St. Paul, MN 55104; (612) 644-1727.

Magazines and Newsletters

Daughters: A Newsletter for Parents of Girls Ages Eight to Eighteen, 1808 Ashwood Ave., Nashville, TN 37212; (800) 829-1088

Equity: Newsletter for the Education of Women and Girls, Marymount Institute for the Education of Women and Girls, Marymount College, 100 Marymount Ave.,Tarrytown, NY 10591; (914) 332-4917

Ms., 135 West 50th St., 16th Floor, New York, NY 10020; (212) 445-6100. Subscriptions: (800) 234-4486

New Moon Network: For Adults Who Care About Girls, P.O. Box 3587, Duluth, MN 55803-3587; (218) 728-5507

Take Action for Girls, Upper Midwest History Center, c/o Hamline University, 1536 Hewitt Ave., Saint Paul, MN 55104

Organizations

American Association of University Women, 1111 16th St. NW, Washington, DC 20036; (202) 785-7700

Association of Teacher Educators, 1900 Association Dr., Suite ATE, Reston, VA 22091-1502; (703) 620-3110

Center for Research on Women, Publications Department, 106 Central St., Wellesley, MA 02181-8259; (617) 283-2510

Consortium for Education Equity, Rutgers University, Building 4090, Livingston Campus, New Brunswick, NJ 08903; (908) 445-2071

The Equals Project, Lawrence Hall of Science, University of California, Berkeley, CA 94720; (510) 642-1823

Girls Count, 225 E. 16th Ave., Suite 475, Denver, CO 80203; (303) 832-6600

Girls Incorporated, National Headquarters, 30 E. 33rd St., New York, NY 10016; (212) 689-3700

Math/Science Network, Mills College, 5000 MacArthur Blvd., Oakland, CA 94613; (510) 430-2222

National Coalition of Girls' Schools, 228 Main St., Concord, MA 01742; (508) 287-4485

National Coalition for Sex Equity in Education, One Redwood Dr., Clifton, NJ, 08809; (908) 735-5045

National Women's History Project, 7738 Bell Rd., Windsor, CA 95492-8518; (707) 838-6000

Resources for Girls and Young Women, 817 Vincente Way, Suite B, Santa Barbara, CA 93105; (805) 569-2398

A Sporting Chance Foundation, 5002 N. Hermitage, Chicago, IL 60640; (312) 784-0820

Women's Educational Equity Act, Publishing Center, 55 Chapel St., Newton, MA 02158-1060; (800) 225-3088

Principal Sources

Chapter 1: Looking Out for #1

American Association of University Women. "Fact Sheet: Shortchanging Girls, Shortchanging America."

Bower, Bruce. "Teenage Turning Point." *Science News* 139–140 (March 23, 1991): 184–186.

Branden, Nathanial. "A Woman's Self-Esteem." *New Woman* (January 1993): 56–58.

Brown, Lynn Mikel, and Carol Gilligan. *Meeting at the Crossroads.* New York: Ballantine Books, 1993.

Brown, Valerie. "Don't Put Up with Putting Yourself Down!" *Teen* 35 (September 1991): 52.

Debold, Elizabeth, Marie Wilson, and Idelisse Malave. *Mother-Daughter Revolution: Good Girls to Great Women.* New York: Bantam, 1994.

Dworkin, Susan. "Can We Save the Girls?" *New Directions for Women* (September/October 1991): 3–4.

Eagle, Carol J., and Carol Colman. *All That She Can Be: Helping Your Daughter Achieve Her Full Potential and Maintain Her Self-Esteem During the Critical Years of Adolescence.* New York: Simon & Schuster, 1993.

"For Our Daughters." *Parenting* (April 1994): 71–96.

Gilligan, Carol, Nona P. Lyons, and Trudy J. Hamner, editors. *Making Connections: The Relational Worlds of Adolescent Girls at Emma Willard School.* Cambridge, Mass.: Harvard University Press, 1990.

Golden, Kristen. "What Do Girls See?" *Ms.* 4 (May/June 1994): 53–61.

Larsen, Elizabeth. "The Great Teen Girl Self-Esteem Robbery." *Utne Reader* (January/February 1992): 20–21.

Steinem, Gloria. *Revolution from Within: A Book of Self-Esteem.* Boston: Little, Brown, 1992.

Stretchberry, Barbara. "Reflections of Risk: An Early Look at Girls' Self-Esteem." *New Moon Parenting* 2 (November/December 1994): 1.

Urbanska, Wanda. "Self-Esteem: The Hope of the Future." *New Woman* (March 1991): 52–56.

Van Gelder, Lindsay. "The Importance of Being Eleven." *Ms.* 1 (July/August 1990): 77–79.

Women's Educational Equity Act Publishing Center. "Building a Self: Teenaged Girls and Issues of Self-Esteem." September 1991.

Chapter 2: Go Figure

Brown, Catrina, and Karin Jasper, editors. *Consuming Passions: Feminist Approaches to Weight Preoccupation and Eating Disorders.* Toronto: Second Story Press, 1993.

Brumberg, Joan Jacobs. *Fasting Girls: The History of Anorexia Nervosa.* New York: New American Library, 1989.

Cauwels, Janice M. *Bulimia: The Binge-Purge Compulsion.* Garden City, N.Y.: Doubleday, 1983.

Hatfield, Elaine, and Susan Sprecher. *Mirror, Mirror: The Importance of Looks in Everyday Life*. Albany: State University of New York Press, 1986.

Kolodny, Nancy J. *When Food's a Foe: How to Confront and Conquer Eating Disorders*. Boston: Little, Brown, 1987.

Landau, Elaine. *Weight: A Teenage Concern*. New York: Lodestar Books, 1991.

Lang, Susan S. "Shape Up Your Body Image." *New Woman* (March 1993): 68–70.

Laskin, David, and Kathleen O'Neill. *The Little Girl Book: Everything You Need to Know to Raise a Daughter Today*. New York: Ballantine, 1992.

Stone, Judith. "He's Just Big—She's Fat." *San Francisco Examiner* (May 10, 1993): D3.

Swensen, Christine L. "What's Normal?" *New Moon* Sample Issue (1993): 27.

"Through the Looking Glass: The 1994 *New Woman* Beauty Survey." *New Woman* (October 1994): 90–95.

Wolf, Naomi. *The Beauty Myth: How Images of Beauty Are Used Against Women*. New York: Anchor, 1992.

Chapter 3: You Go, Girl!

Buchsbaum, Herbert. "Revolution, Girl Style." *Scholastic Update* 125 (March 12, 1993): 22–23.

Chideya, Farai, with Melissa Rossi and Dogen Hannah. "Revolution, Girl Style." *Newsweek* 120 (November 23, 1992): 84–86.

Hancock, Emily. "Growing Up Female." *New Woman* (May 1993): 82.

———. *The Girl Within*. New York: Fawcett Columbine, 1989.

King, Laurel. *A Whistling Woman Is Up to No Good: Finding Your Wild Woman*. Berkeley, Calif.: Celestial Arts, 1993.

Stemmermann, Joann. "The Courage to Just Do It: Girls & Experience-Based Learning." *New Moon Parenting* 1 (November/December 1993): 1.

Chapter 4: Good Housekeeping

Hochschild, Arlie, with Anne Machung. *The Second Shift: Working Parents and the Revolution at Home*. New York: Avon, 1990.

Mann, Judy. *The Difference: Growing Up Female in America*. New York: Warner, 1994.

Mainardi, Pat. "The Politics of Housework," in *Sisterhood Is Powerful*, by Robin Morgan. New York: Random House, 1970.

Robinson, John P. "The Hard Facts About Hard Work." *Utne Reader* (March/April 1990): 70.

Sachs, Jessica. "Mind & Body." *New Woman* (March 1991): 150.

Sward, Susan. "Experts Say Wives-as-Property Still a Common U.S. Attitude." *San Francisco Chronicle* (August 1, 1994): A13.

Taylor, Debbie. "Domestic Chores Weren't Always Women's Work." *Utne Reader* (March/April 1990): 80–81.

York, Lyle. "Who Does the Housework?" *San Francisco Chronicle* (February 24, 1993): Z1.

Chapter 5: Take That!

Dee, Catherine, editor, and the EarthWorks Group. *The Woman's Guide to Political Power*. Berkeley, Calif.: EarthWorks Press, 1993.

King County Sexual Assault Resource Center

Levy, Barrie. *In Love & In Danger: A Teen's Guide to Breaking Free of Abusive Relationships*. Seattle: Seal Press, 1992.

National Crime Prevention Council
Women's Educational Equity Act Publishing Center. "Educating Against Gender-Based Violence."
October 1992.

Chapter 6: Class Acts

Bailey, Susan McGee, Center for Research on Women, Wellesley College. "In the Interest of All: Achieving Sex Equity in Education." 1991.

DeCrow, Karen. *The Young Woman's Guide to Liberation: Alternatives to a Half-Life While the Choice Is Still Yours.* New York: Pegasus, 1971.

Gersoni-Stavn, Diane. *Sexism and Youth.* New York: Bowker, 1974.

Kaplan, Lisa Faye. "Reading Between the Lines: Women's Images in Children's Books." Gannett News Service, n.d.

Kelly, Joe. "Dr. Myra Sadker: Gender Equity Pioneer." *New Moon Parenting* 1 (July/August 1994): 1.

Laskin, David, and Kathleen O'Neill. *The Little Girl Book: Everything You Need to Know to Raise a Daughter Today.* New York: Ballantine, 1992.

Logan, Judy. *Teaching Stories.* St. Paul: Minnesota Inclusiveness Program, 1993.

Orenstein, Peggy. *Schoolgirls: Young Women, Self-Esteem, and the Confidence Gap.* New York: Doubleday, 1994.

———."The Reader's Companion to *Schoolgirls.*" 1994.

Sadker, Myra and David. *Failing at Fairness: How America's Schools Cheat Girls.* New York: Scribner's, 1994.

Ward, Tya. "Feminist Teacher Doug Kirkpatrick: Overcoming Bias." *New Moon Parenting* 2 (January/February 1995): 9.

Weitzman, Lenore J. "Sex Role Socialization: A Focus on Women," in *Women: A Feminist Perspective,* edited by Jo Freeman. Mountain View, Calif.: Mayfield Publishing Co., 1989.

Chapter 7: Math Myths and Science Fiction

American Association of University Women Educational Foundation. "The AAUW Report: How Schools Shortchange Girls." 1992.

Borowitz, Susan D., ed. "Math/Science Network Broadcast." Math/Science Network, summer 1994.

Evenson, Laura. "Video-Game Makers Target Girls." *San Francisco Chronicle* (June 27, 1994): D1.

Examiner News Services. "Girls Lag in Science Past 4th Grade." *San Francisco Examiner* (March 27, 1992): A12.

Flores, Deborah. "Why Girls Don't Excel in Math." *Parents Press* (September 1992): 13–14.

Fryer, Bronwyn. "Games for Girls in a Gameboy World." *Working Woman* 19 (December 1994): 11.

Laskin, David, and Kathleen O'Neill. *The Little Girl Book: Everything You Need to Know to Raise a Daughter Today.* New York: Ballantine, 1992.

"Men, Women & Computers." *Newsweek* 123 (May 16, 1994): 48–53.

Sadker, Myra and David. *Failing at Fairness: How America's Schools Cheat Girls.* New York: Scribner's, 1994.

Women's Educational Equity Act Publishing Center. "Girls and Math: Enough Is Known for Action." June 1991.

Chapter 8: Leave Me Alone!

American Association of University Women Educational Foundation. "The AAUW Report: How Schools Shortchange Girls." 1992.

———."Shortchanging Girls, Shortchanging America: Executive Summary." 1994.

Blashfield, Jean. *Hellraisers, Heroines, and Holy Women: Women's Most Remarkable Contributions to History*. New York: St. Martin's, 1981.

"Girls' Victory in Harassment Suit Came at a Price." *San Francisco Chronicle* (October 3, 1996): A17.

Harris/Scholastic Research in partnership with Scholastic Inc. *Hostile Hallways: The AAUW Survey on Sexual Harassment in America's Schools*. 1993.

Hodgson, Harriet. *Power Plays: How Teens Can Pull the Plug on Sexual Harassment*. Minneapolis: Deaconess, 1993.

Lanpher, Katherine. "Reading, 'Riting, and 'Rassment." *Ms.* 2 (May/June 1992): 90.

NOW Legal Defense and Education Fund. "Legal Resource Kit: Sexual Harassment in the Schools." 1992.

Programs for Educational Opportunity, University of Michigan. "Tune In to Your Rights: A Guide for Teenagers About Turning Off Sexual Harassment." 1985.

Saltzman, Amy. "It's Not Just Teasing." *U.S. News & World Report* 115 (December 6, 1993): 73–77.

Sauerwein, Kristina. "A New Lesson in Schools: Sexual Harassment Is Unacceptable." *Los Angeles Times* 113 (August 1, 1994): E1.

Spaid, Elizabeth Levitan. "Sexual Harassment Found in U.S. Schools." *Christian Science Monitor* 85 (June 2, 1993): 7.

Strauss, Susan. *Sexual Harassment and Teens: A Program for Positive Change*. Minneapolis: Free Spirit, 1992.

Chapter 9: Know the Score

Aburdene, Patricia, and John Naisbitt. *Megatrends for Women*. New York: Villard, 1992.

"Are Men Taking Over Women's Sports?" *Glamour* 89 (September 1991): 119.

Day, Brenda. "Not All Sugar and Spice." *Los Angeles Times* 113 (January 4, 1994): A3

Irwin, Victoria. "Shooting for Equality." *Scholastic Update* 124 (May 1, 1992): 24–25.

Mann, Judy. *The Difference: Growing Up Female in America*. New York: Warner, 1994.

Reith, Kathryn. "Leveling the Field." *Women's Sports & Fitness* 14 (April 1992): 90.

Shannon, Jacqueline. *Why It's Great to Be a Girl*. New York: Warner, 1994.

Wilson Sporting Goods Co. and Women's Sports Foundation. "The Wilson Report: Moms, Dads, Daughters and Sports." 1988.

Women's Educational Equity Act Publishing Center. "Games Yet to Be Played: Equity in Sport Leadership." June 1994.

Chapter 10: Media Darling

Bingham, Mindy, Judy Edmondson, and Sandy Stryker. *Choices: A Teen Woman's Journal for Self-Awareness and Personal Planning*. Santa Barbara, Calif.: Advocacy Press, 1983.

Bridge, M. Junior. "Slipping from the Scene." 1995.

Carter, Bill. "Children's TV, Where Boys Are King." *New York Times* 140 (May 1, 1991): A1.

Center for Media Literacy. "Break the Lies that Bind: Sexism in the Media." 1994.

Douglas, Susan J. *Where the Girls Are: Growing Up Female with the Mass Media*. New York: Times Books, 1994.

Dunn, Rita, and Kenneth Dunn. *How to Raise Independent and Professionally Successful Daughters*. Englewood Cliffs, N.J.: Prentice Hall, 1977.

Gibbons, Sheila, ed. "Media Report to Women: The Newsletter Covering All the Issues Concerning Women and Media" 23 (summer 1995).

Girls Incorporated. "Girls Re-Cast TV," 1994.

Kelly, Caitlin. "The Great Paper Chase." *Ms.* 3 (May/June 1993): 34–35.

Levitt, Shelley. "Does TV Shortchange Teenage Girls?" *TV Guide* 40 (July 11, 1992): 12–13.

Marin, Rick. "TV's Trouble with Teens." *TV Guide* 42 (March 12, 1994): 36–37.

Media Action Resource Center. *Media & Values: Redesigning Women* 49 (winter 1989).

Media Watch. "Action Agenda" selected issues.

National Commission on Working Women of Wider Opportunities for Women. "What's Wrong with this Picture? The Status of Women On Screen and Behind the Camera in Entertainment TV." 1990.

Pipher, Mary. *Reviving Ophelia: Saving the Selves of Adolescent Girls.* New York: Putman, 1994.

Screen Actors Guild. "Women and Minorities on Television." 1993.

Wolf, Naomi. *Fire with Fire: The New Female Power and How It Will Change the 21st Century.* New York: Random House, 1993.

Women, Men & Media

Chapter 11: The "Old Boys' Club"

Aburdene, Patricia, and John Naisbitt. *Megatrends for Women.* New York: Villard, 1992.

Blashfield, Jean. *Hellraisers, Heroines, and Holy Women: Women's Most Remarkable Contributions to History.* New York: St. Martin's, 1981.

Catalyst. "Women in Government Fact Sheet." 1995.

Center for the American Woman and Politics, Rutgers University

Dee, Catherine, editor, and the EarthWorks Group. *The Woman's Guide to Political Power.* Berkeley, Calif.: EarthWorks Press, 1993.

DiMona, Lisa, and Constance Herndon, editors. *The 1995 Information Please Women's Sourcebook.* New York: Houghton Mifflin, 1994.

Henry, Sherrye. "Why Women Don't Vote for Women and Why They Should." *Working Woman* 19 (June 1994): 49–52, 86.

Martin, Lynn. "Still a Boys' Club." *New York Times* 142 (January 23, 1993): 21.

National Women's Political Caucus

Riordan, Teresa, and Sue Kirchhoff. "Women on the Hill: Can They Make a Difference?" *Ms.* 5 (January/February 1995): 85–90.

Chapter 12: Spread the Word

Crawford, Susan H. *Beyond Dolls & Guns: 101 Ways to Help Children Avoid Gender Bias.* Portsmouth, N.H.: Heinemann, 1995.

Erens, Pamela. "Gender-Biased Men." *Glamour* 90 (June 1992).

Harding, Cathryn. "Pink and Blue Pronouns." *Parenting* 6 (April 1992): 45–46.

Miller, Casey, and Kate Swift. *Words and Women.* Garden City, New York: Anchor Press/Doubleday, 1976.

Penelope, Julia. *Speaking Freely: Unlearning the Lies of the Fathers' Tongues.* New York: Teachers College Press, 1990.

Popović, Neil A. F. "The Game of the Name." *Ms.* 5 (November/December 1994): 96.

St. Louis County NOW. *A Practical Guide to Non-Sexist Language.* 1995.

Vetterling-Braggin, Mary. *Sexist Language: A Modern Philosophical Analysis.* Lanham, Md.: Rowman and Littlefield, 1981.

Chapter 13: Selling Us Short

Clark, Eric. *The Want Makers: Inside the World of Advertising.* New York: Viking, 1989.

Communication Research Associates. *Media Report to Women* 23 (summer 1995).

Feinsilber, Mike. "Psychologists Say TV Ignores All but Young Buying Public." *San Francisco Examiner* (February 1992).

Horovitz, Bruce. "Lucrative Side of Teen-Age Anxieties." *Los Angeles Times* 111 (October 4, 1992): D1.

Jackson, Donna. *How to Make the World a Better Place for Women in 5 Minutes a Day.* New York: Hyperion, 1992.

Media Action Resource Center. *Media & Values: Redesigning Women* 49 (winter 1989).

Media Watch. "Action Agenda," selected issues.

Morgan, Robin. *Sisterhood Is Powerful.* New York: Random House, 1970.

Chapter 14: Creative Differences

Antrobe, Helen. "Revolution Girl-Style Now!" *Utne Reader* (March/April 1993): 17–18.

"Briefing: The Old Boy Network." *New Woman* (March 1991): 26.

Broude, Norma, and Mary D. Garrard. *The Power of Feminist Art: The American Movement of the 1970s, History and Impact.* New York: Abrams, 1994.

Burnham, Sophy. "Portrait of the Artist as a Woman." *New Woman* (June 1990): 94.

"Female Moviegoers Make 'Wives' a Hit." *Washington Post* (October 1, 1996): D7.

Gillespie, Marcia Ann. "Guerrilla Girls: From Broadsides to Broadsheets." *Ms.* 3 (March/April 1993): 69.

Heller, Nancy G. *Women Artists: An Illustrated History.* New York: Abbeville, 1987.

National Museum of Women in the Arts

O'Neil, Kerry. "Striking at Sexism in the Art World." *Christian Science Monitor* 83 (December 17, 1990): 10.

"Selected Highlights from the Feminist Art Movement." *Ms.* 3 (July/August 1992): 68–72.

Chapter 15: Working Woman

Cinereski, Stephanie. "Succeeding in Science." *New Moon* 2 (May/June 1995): 37.

Godfrey, Joline. "What About Girls?" *At Work* (March/April 1994): 3–5.

Howard, Beth. "A Day for Women." *Self* (March 1995): 76.

Noble, Barbara Presley. "When Daughters Invade the Office." *New York Times* (April 4, 1993): 25.

Nussbaum, Karen. "Removing Barriers for Working Women." *Christian Science Monitor* (March 24, 1994): 19.

"They're Beginning to Look a Lot Like Sexists." *Working Woman* 19 (December 1994): 29.

U.S. Department of Labor. "Working Women Count!: A Report to the Nation." 1994.

"Women Managers Trump Men in Survey on Leadership Skills." *San Francisco Examiner* (September 19, 1996): 1.

Women's Research Education Institute. *The American Woman 1992–1993.* New York: Norton, 1993.

Woodruff, Virginia. "Working Girls." *Working Woman* 19 (March 1994): 11–12.

Index

Copyright Acknowledgments

Maya Angelou: "Phenomenal Woman" from *And Still I Rise* by Maya Angelou. Copyright © 1978 by Maya Angelou. Reprinted by permission of Random House, Inc.

Robin Beran: "Math Notes" by Robin Beran from *New Moon: The Magazine for Girls and Their Dreams*, July/August 1994. Reprinted by permission of New Moon Publishing.

Kathy Bowen-Woodward: "The Gardener and the Tree" from *Coping with a Negative Body Image* by Kathy Bowen-Woodward. Reprinted by permission of Rosen Publishing Group.

Brazley Daraja: "My Brother Does Dishes" by Brazley Daraja. Copyright © by Brazley Daraja. Reprinted by permission of the author.

Danial Dunlap: "How I Fought Back" by Danial Dunlap. Copyright © by Danial Dunlap. Reprinted by permission of the author.

JoAnn Falletta: "Leader of the Band" by JoAnn Falletta from *Women and Work: In Their Own Words*, edited by Maureen R. Michelson. Reprinted by permission of New Sage Press.

Andrea Floyd: "Climbing Lessons" by Andrea Floyd. Copyright © by Andrea Floyd. Reprinted by permission of the author.

Susan Gillette: "Truths About Advertising" by Susan Gillette. Copyright © by Susan Gillette. Reprinted by permission of the author.

"Girls Go After the Ads" letter excerpts. Copyright © by the Girl Scouts–Illinois Crossroads Council. Reprinted by permission of Girl Scouts–Illinois Crossroads Council.

Josh Haner: "Thank You, Ms. Logan" by Josh Haner. Copyright © by Josh Haner. Reprinted by permission of the author.

Sheldon Harnick: "Housework" by Sheldon Harnick, from *Free to Be...You & Me* by Marlo Thomas and Friends. Copyright © 1974 by Free to Be Foundation, Inc. Reprinted by permission of Free to Be Foundation, Inc.

Brooke Hodess: "Finding Your Voice" by Brooke Hodess. Copyright © by Brooke Hodess. Reprinted by permission of the author.

Sarah Duff Harris: "Gender Inequity" by Sarah Duff Harris. Copyright © by Sarah Duff Harris. Reprinted by permission of the author.

Maggie Jones: "A Goal for the Girls" by Maggie Jones first appeared in the article "Smart Cookies" in *Working Woman*, April 1995. Copyright © 1995 by *Working Woman* Magazine. Reprinted by permission of *Working Woman* Magazine.

Jane Garland Katz: "Write a Letter" adapted from "Write a Letter to the Editor" by Jane Garland Katz from *50/50 by 2000: The Woman's Guide to Political Power*. Reprinted by permission of Earthworks Press.

Amanda Keller: "A Girl's Place Is in the House" by Amanda Keller. Copyright © by Amanda Keller. Reprinted by permission of the author.

Doug Kirkpatrick: "The Joy of Science" by Doug Kirkpatrick. Copyright © by Doug Kirkpatrick. Reprinted by permission of the author.